# So You Want to
# Go to College!

D1715824

Other books co-authored by Professor Pinkerton:

*Supply Management,* 8th ed.
David N. Burt, Sheila D. Petcavage and Richard L. Pinkerton, Burr
Ridge, IL, McGraw-Hill Irwin, 2010. ISBN 978-0-07-338145-9

*A Purchasing Manager's Guide to Strategic Proactive Procurement*
David N. Burt and Richard L. Pinkerton, NY, NY. The American
Management Association (AMACOM) 1996. ISBN 0-8144-0288-7

# So You Want to Go to College!

## Richard LaDoyt Pinkerton, Ph. D.

Professor Pinkerton's Guide
for high school students to help answer questions such
as: are you ready, what to study, where to go, where
to live, how to successfully get your degree and what
happens after commencement.

**VANTAGE**Press
New York

Vantage Press and the Vantage Press colophon
are registered trademarks of Vantage Press, Inc.

FIRST EDITION

Copyright © 2011 by  Richard LaDoyt Pinkerton, Ph.D.

Published by Vantage Press, Inc.
419 Park Ave. South, New York, NY 10016

Manufactured in the United States of America
ISBN: 978-0-533-16346-5

Library of Congress Catalog Card No: 2010921680

0 9 8 7 6 5 4 3 2 1

To all of my former students
who always inspired me with their questions, work, creativity
and quest
for improving our great country.

# Contents

# Acknowledgments

Many thanks to Trish Sharp and Steve Shawver at Minuteman Press in Strongsville, Ohio, for their patience, skill, and support at the word processor, just as they did on my textbook, *Supply Management*. Robert Skully, an experienced high school teacher in the Cleveland, area, was a valuable reviewer, as was Strongsville, Ohio, high school student Gillian Maxfield. A former Air Force buddy, Lt. Col. Bryon Nelson, USAF (retired), offered good advice. Also, thanks to my wonderful daughters, Elizabeth and Patricia, both college graduates but still young enough to offer good advice. Thanks also go to Professor Kelly Webb, technical writing instructor at the University of Akron, Ohio; and Professor Sheila Petcavage of Cuyahoga Community College in Cleveland, Ohio, and one of my coauthors of *Supply Management* (McGraw-Hill/Irwin). Both Professors reinforced many of my thoughts expressed in this book. A longtime friend, Cathryn Buesseler, retired Professor of Journalism at Texas Tech University in Lubbock, also helped with editing. Finally, longtime high school guidance counselor, Julia Williams, offered invaluable advice.

# Introduction

This guidebook is primarily written for high school students contemplating going to college for their first degree, the bachelors. It should also prove very useful for parents and high school counselors. My thoughts are based on my forty-five years of counseling and teaching experience at a Big Ten school, Wisconsin; a private school, Capital University, in Columbus, Ohio; and California State University, Fresno. While it is currently politically correct to suggest that all high school graduates go on to college, I suspect there is not one college professor who believes these assertions by politicians, many parents, and some high school counselors.

The book starts with a chapter written strictly for you, by asking a key question: Are *you* willing, able, and ready to attempt higher education? Do not confuse this question with the universal need for training, a requirement for all of us in the workforce. My hope is that you find this book especially helpful for the first step: to go or not to go. For the next decision steps I include chapters on what to study, where to go, where to live, surviving the challenge, and maximizing the value of the experience. I conclude with a short chapter on commencement and life after college.

Remember, your parents and/or other relatives and supporters want what they think is best for you and, while they mean well, you must pursue your life's dreams that fit your ability, desire, and goals. I have counseled many college students who hated the college experience and wanted to do something else with their lives. If you want to be a welder, go for it! By the way, society needs good welders, probably more than we need graduates in many subjects. A recent statement from a blog says it very well:

"College isn't for all. Forcing all high school students into a college education is not only wrong, it's dumb. Our nation needs blue-collar workers—skilled mechanics, machinists, carpenters, and computer technicians—just as much as it needs college grads."

However, we do not go to college simply to earn a better living—more on this thought in Chapter One.

Each chapter is in the form of a lecture, so imagine yourself in my college orientation class, filled with lists of questions, advice, and pointers—somewhat like PowerPoint presentations. The class bell is ringing, so please come into my classroom...

# About the Professor

Richard L. Pinkerton is Professor Emeritus of Marketing and Logistics at California State University in Fresno (CSUF). He received his B.A. In Economics from the University of Michigan in Ann Arbor, his M.B.A. From Case Western Reserve University in Cleveland, Ohio, and a Ph. D. in marketing and Curriculum Studies from the University of Wisconsin, Madison.

After receiving his Ph. D., for several years he taught marketing in the School of Business at Wisconsin, where he was the faculty advisor to the Student Marketing Club and the social fraternity of Phi Gamma Delta. He also was the coach for the Intercollegiate Marketing Team that placed second two years in a row at the Michigan State University finals of the Computer Simulation Marketing Competition. Professor Pinkerton then joined Capital University, a private Lutheran Institution in Columbus, Ohio, as the Founding Dean of the Graduate School of Administration, where he also taught sales management and purchasing. He served Capital from 1974 to 1986, after which he was selected to be a Professor and Director at the Business Center at the Craig School of Business at California State University in Fresno, California (CSUF). He was later elected as chair of the Department of Marketing and Logistics. During his tenure at CSUF, or "Fresno State," as the athletic teams are called, he became a noted scholar, consultant, teacher, and researcher in the field of marketing intelligence, supply-chain management, and purchasing. He combined his academic experience with his previous industrial experience at the Harris Corporation, where he was a market research analyst, and at the Webb-Triax Company, where he was manager of sales development, to become a popular advisor to several student clubs and associations.

He received awards from the Hmong Student Association (Vietnamese Students), the Hispanic Business Student Association, the Alpha Kappa Psi National Business Fraternity, and the social fraternity of Phi Gamma Delta. In addition, he was a long-time faculty mentor in the Disadvantaged Student Counseling Program and an advisor to prospective students in the California High-School-to-Career Interstate 5 Business Development Corridor project, advising program team members who visited major rural high schools in the San Joaquin Valley.

A former high school football player, he also served as a faculty admissions counselor for the Fresno State "Bulldog" football team. He also served for many years as one of the original faculty members in the CSUF Craig School of Business Honors Program. In his travels as a guest professor in London, Singapore, Germany, Poland, Chile, Saudi Arabia, and Slovakia, Dr. Pinkerton gained vast experience about global students and American students studying abroad. The recipient of many awards, in 2002 he was honored to receive the Ted R. Thompson Award from the Columbus, Ohio, Purchasing Society for his contributions to purchasing education. A retired Lt. Col. in the USAF Ready Reserves, he holds the Meritorious Service Medal for his many years of military leadership. Dr. Pinkerton has been listed in *Who's Who of America* since 1982.

As a former BMOC ('big man on campus') at the University of Michigan, Professor Pinkerton advocates extracurricular activities as "the other fifty percent of the education value." His fellow students elected him as the student commencement speaker at the June 11, 1955, University of Michigan commencement ceremony in the great Michigan Stadium in Ann Arbor. The following "campus profile" appeared in the October 16, 1954, issue of the *Michigan Alumnus* magazine.

Richard L. Pinkerton, '55, fiftieth Executive Secretary of the Union and number two man on its Board of Directors, not only keeps busy as Business manager of the student office of the Union, but has his hand in many other organizations and activities. He entered Michigan from Parma Schaaf High School, Parma, Ohio, where he had been in varsity football and track, in addition to serving as Student City Manager. After a stint as an Air Force second Lieutenant he plans to return to law school. Dick, an active debater, won the state junior division in the Hearst Newspapers' Tournament of Orators, which was held in Detroit in 1953. Other activities include membership in Michigamua, Arnold Air Society, Scabbard and Blade, and Phi Gamma Delta. Academically, he majors in economics, but is seriously interested in civil war history.

Professor Pinkerton has a unique background and his rare combination of industry, military, and academic experience, including more than forty-five years of counseling experience, makes this a very special guidebook for prospective college students. Professor Pinkerton is still active in civic activities in his hometown of Cleveland, where he now resides in the suburb of Strongsville. He has two adult daughters: Patricia E. Pinkerton, a registered dietitian and a sports trainer in Vallejo, California, and Elizabeth L. Pinkerton, the events coordinator for the University of Wisconsin Health System in Madison, Wisconsin.

# So You Want to Go to College!

# 1

# Are You Ready, Able, and Willing to Go to College?

For the small number of you who have received some kind of merit scholarship to the school of your choice, you can probably skip this chapter and move to selected later chapters. Obviously, you know you are going to college and where.

Otherwise, the question to ask yourself is, "Are you ready to learn at the next level?" If you are not commuting, the other question is, "For the moment, are you also ready to leave home?" College is the first true break from the warmth and safety of your home, assuming you come from a reasonably functional home. I went to college with several orphans who seemed well prepared to be on their own, simply because they had to be independent.

First, the issue of grade creep—grade inflation—must be addressed. Over the last forty years or so, there have been trends at all education levels to reduce the grading standards (rigor), which has resulted in higher-than-normal GPAs, "B" means bad. One indicator of this trend is the ever increasing number of perfect 4.00 students graduating from high school and college. So what? The response is, you might not be as smart as you think you are. The result is, you run the risk of being shocked to discover, from a tough professor, that you are not the grade-A English student you thought you were, when confronted with higher standards, and increased competition from your classmates in college. The case of Kristin Segerson is a good example of college grade shock. In her words:

In high school ... I was a straight "A" student. I had been accepted to Miami University in Ohio. I first realized I was struggling after I began my freshman year ... and by my sophomore year, my grade-point average was down to roughly a 2.6, despite a lot of effort.[1]

Expect to be challenged—that's what college is all about. None of us have the right to win anything, but we do have the right to compete. No one automatically deserves a college degree, it must be earned.

See how you score on my following simple quiz designed to give some indication of whether or not you are prepared to run off to the college of your choice. Note that there is no total score, just a + or − with the + answers suggesting you are ready; the more +'s, the better. Please note that this test is to see if you are ready to attend the traditional four-year college, not if you're capable of enrolling at vocational schools, community colleges, and other technical institutes. Caution: try to avoid giving what you think is the proper response—that is, be true to yourself.

Here is my test on your potential to be a successful college student:

1. Do you have intellectual curiosity? Do you wonder what makes people, things, institutions, ideas, countries, etc., work and why?

---

1.  Bill Yurgen, "Learning Rx Success Stories: Second In A Series, 'Where Are They Now.'" Brunswick, Ohio, Mimi Vanderhaven. November 19, 2009, p. 49, www.mimivanderhaven.com. Note: Learning Rx is a cognitive training program; see LearningRx.com. For a good discussion of grade inflation, see *Dumbing Down Our Kids: Why American Children Feel Good About Themselves But Can't Read, Write, or Add,* by Charles J. Sykes, New York, N.Y., St. Martin's Griffin, 1995. pp. 3, 10, 30–32, 65, 71, 96, 221, 291, 294, and *The Lowering of Higher Education in America: Why Financial Aid Should Be Based on Student Performance,* by Jackson Toby, Santa Barbara, California, Praeger, an Imprint of ABC-CLIO, LLC, 2010, pp. 65–89.

2. Are you competitive? Can you keep going when the situation gets tough or do you quit?
3. Are you coachable? Are you a good listener and receptive to constructive criticism?
4. Part of number 3—do you have very thin skin, are you highly defensive? If you think you are right most of the time, you are not ready to study and react to proper criticism.
5. Do you like to read books? If the answer is no, forget about college. Reading is the key to mastering language, grammar, construction, improving your vocabulary, and it stimulates intellectual exercise and development. The Internet and computer online information are very useful, but not nearly the same, nor as powerful. Much of the computer data is abbreviated English, incomplete, often false, and undocumented.[2]
6. Do you like to visit libraries? Do you like that atmosphere?
7. Do you occasionally like to browse in a bookstore?
8. Are you self-disciplined? Do you know when to play and when to work? Can you stick to a task until its completion? Typical college tasks are reading assignments, completing papers, working and solving problems, finishing projects, laboratory work, practicing, searching the Internet, researching in the library, going on field trips, and a multitude of various other tasks. So how is it different from high school? It's very simple, you are largely on your own to complete these tasks—no parents or readily available counselors—and most of the faculty

---

2. Many university faculty members make this same statement. For example, see *Academe Online: An Open Letter to Ninth Graders*, by Patrick Sullivan, coauthor of *What is "College-level" Writing*, with Howard Tinberg, ISBN 978-0-8141-5674-2, National Council of Teachers' of English (NCTE), Urbana, IL, 2006. See www.aaup.org/pubsres/academe/2009.

will hold you to deadlines. In short, for the most part, you are on your own.

9. Do museums interest you?
10. Do you have a sense of adventure?—because that's what college is.
11. Do you like to write?—because college is all about writing. The more you write, the greater your opportunity to improve your vocabulary, analytical reasoning, logical thinking pattern, persuasion skills, and the overall ability to correctly express yourself. Unfortunately, the speed and ease of e-mails and Twitter has produced an epidemic of atrocious English shorthand and "texting" without thinking.[3] By the way, good writers are usually avid readers, and vice versa.
12. Are you a good verbal communicator, and do you feel comfortable giving oral reports in front of an audience?
13. Do you like history? Learning where we have been helps us to know where we are going, and it is another good intellectual exercise.
14. When you watch TV, do you ever watch the History Channel and/or the Discovery Channel?
15. Do you ever watch the Public Broadcasting Channel?
16. Are you physically and mentally healthy enough to run around a campus, study, and cope with stress?
17. How did you like high school? No one likes everything about high school but if you really hated school, you are not ready for college, unless you are truly gifted and were bored.
18. Do you "regularly" read a newspaper? Unfortunately, we know that few high school students read newspapers. As you read the many references from newspapers quoted in this book, I hope this stimulates you to read at

---

3. Ibid.

least one major newspaper. Neither the Internet nor TV can provide you with the same detailed information, in real depth beyond the headlines.

19. Do you like at least some classical music, and do you ever go to a symphony concert?
20. Do you ever go to stage plays, such as dramas or Broadway musicals?
21. Are you excited about at least a few basic disciplines such as art, math, chemistry, music, history, literature, science, psychology, philosophy, law, medicine, teaching, business, engineering?
22. Are you a good listener? You can't learn if you can't hear and understand instructions, explanations, facts, opinions, questions, and the like,[4] Remember, Mother Nature gave us two ears and just one mouth.

Well, how did you score, how many +'s? Few individuals would be able to say "yes" to all of the questions. Even if you did not have a + for an area, if you have an interest to try the activity, that's a good sign. If you were perfect in all categories, you would not need college. In other words, just because you like to write, it doesn't mean you don't need further practice and/or that you are A+ on the topic. Notice, I often used the word "like," and we usually like what we are good at, and vice versa.

If you are addicted to passive entertainment such as iPods and TV, you are probably not ready for college. Such activities are pure entertainment and I think too much TV could contribute to brain numbness.

Aside from ability and interests, what we are really talking about is maturity. Are you adult enough to live and study on your own, with only nominal supervision? For example, if you need your mother or father to walk you through registration, you are not

---

4. Ibid.

5

ready for college. If your mother is the classic "helicopter mom," you should not need this kind of security. Gently suggest that she let go. While it's perfectly normal for parents to help their kids move into the dorm, they can't go to school for them.

My experience tells me that most high school seniors know if they are ready for the next level. If you are not sure, ask the advice of a trusted high school counselor, teacher, and/or some intelligent family member for an objective assessment. Ask only those who have gone to college, at least one year, as people who have never attended can't help you—they don't know anything about the college experience, even though many "think they know," which is even more dangerous.

If you are not ready, will you ever be and when will you know it? Most college professors will tell you that many high school seniors are still too young and immature to wander off to college. Many parents and counselors believe that in a perfect world, we would have the typical high school student graduate and then complete two years of community service and/or the military, prior to staring the four-year college. We adults—in particular, parents of both sexes—also know that the girls are usually about four to five years ahead of the boys in maturity (I'm sorry, guys), but does this mean only girls should start right after high school? Of course not, but most adults feel, "I've got to get Carol or Bob into college—right now, before it's too late." Part of this fear is the potential for early marriage and/or parenthood, which indeed does restrict, for many years, the choice/freedom to go to college, and many other major options in life. However, having taught many older entering, and older reentering students, the real answer is, if you are able, you could start and/or finish college at almost any reasonable age. Most professors welcome older students because they are much more motivated to succeed, and know what they want to study, versus the traditional seventeen to eighteen-year-old. Besides, with people living longer, why force yourself to make premature lifelong decision? Part of the answer is that all too often, your mom and dad want you to do what they did not accomplish. Remember Little League Baseball that we all know exists for the parents, not the kids. We also know politicians who love their battle cry of "Let's get them all into college" (off our streets and out of trouble).

But what about those college placement tests, such as the SATs and the ACTs? Aren't they foolproof? The answer is no. They tell something about one's aptitude, academic potential, and ability, but zero about maturity, motivation, energy level, and social skills. A fair number of high-scoring SAT and ACT students quit, flunked out, or never went to college, so we always come back to the real question, "Are *you* ready?"[5] Many experienced high school counselors, and college admissions officials, think participation in extracurricular activities is a better predictor of college success than test scores.[6] I think the reason for this observation is that high school students who volunteer to "do something extra" have more confidence, energy, social skills, and are more competitive than those students who only go to class.

You or your parents might want to engage the services of a college advisor/consultant. These professionals help develop strategies (plans) as to where to apply, how to do it, and how to finance your education. Just make sure you select a legitimate consultant who is accredited with the Certified College Planning Specialist (CCPS) designation, and is a member of the Independent Educational Consultants Association (IECA), and/or the Higher Education Consultants Association (HECA). I will discuss this topic again in later chapters. There are unscrupulous people disguising themselves as consultants, who in reality are trying to sell insurance or investments. Having said this, I still must emphasize that

5. Kim Clark, "Who Will Get Through College?" *US News and World Report*, January 2010, p. 56. Visit www.usnews.com/college.
6. Personal interview with Rea Cantwell, an educational consultant, and the retired principal of Strongsville High School, Strongsville, OH, October 18, 2009.

you must work with them and your parents, throughout the application process so that you understand and have the major input of what you are going to study, where, and how you and your family will pay for your education.

You should begin your search no later than during your sophomore year of high school, in order to allow sufficient time to visit particular colleges, and to take the appropriate preparation courses for the SAT and ACT tests. You will also need time to take the various vocational interest assessment tests, and to research the various career-planning resources, such as *Next Step* magazine's "Career Selection Guides" (see www.nextstepmagazine.com, and see www.careership.com).

I think it is appropriate here to ask yourself, "Why do it?" We go to college for some very basic reasons, like joining professions, such as law, medicine, engineering, science, and education that requires the bachelor's degree, as the entry ticket to further study. Beyond this fact is the idea that college life (notice the word "life") compresses life's experiences to give its graduates an advantage, in not only earning more (which it does), but also in learning how to think critically, which includes problem solving, developing better judgment, and an appreciation for art, history, etc. Educators also hope to produce graduates who will be civic leaders to help build a better country. The real bonus for you is that most college graduates seem to lead more enjoyable and productive lives. Perhaps equally as important, the degree is a door-opener and insurance when the appointment decision is, "Other things being equal." Many employers hire college graduates simply because it demonstrates their discipline and the ability to complete a rather difficult objective. They also feel these graduates will be more "trainable."

Dr. Barbara R. Snyder, president of Case Western Reserve University in Cleveland, Ohio, puts the total value of a college education in the correct perspective, when she states, "Remember, a college education involves far more than work in classrooms and laboratories. Students learn critical skills in leading campus

8

organizations, participating in athletics or performing arts and volunteering in their communities."[7]

Perhaps the proper way to end this opening chapter is to make what might seem to be a wild statement. You do not have to go to college to be a success. I define success as striving for being the very best in what you are capable of achieving and like to do. If you are a carpenter, be the very best carpenter you can be. This is a respected skill needed by all societies, and it provides a respected and comfortable life. The same can be said of firefighters, police, military personnel, printers, machinists, welders, repair technicians, and many others.

I have a dear friend from my high school days, James Bartel, who joined the Air Force after we graduated. After a solid career in Germany as an USAF air controller, he went on to serve as a distinguished civilian air controller, which included the duty of air controller of the National Air Shows, held annually in Cleveland. He was also selected to be the air controller at the internationally known War Bird Annual Air Shows, in Oshkosh, Wisconsin. After retiring from this exciting profession, he became a successful real estate salesman, and he, and his wife, Carol, still serves his city in various civic organizations. The Bartels raised three very successful children and live a very comfortable life. For many people, "success" merely means how much money one makes, how many adults toys they accumulate, and how famous one becomes. For me, success means what you did to earn your assets, did you make a real contribution to society and did you pay back your community, state, and nation with significant contributions?

I believe it is the Bartels of the world and others like them, such as Ronald and Patricia Hutchings (other high school buddies of mine), who help improve their communities, that are the true success stories, not the rich and famous. Ronald Hutchings became a fire chief and, with the help of his wife Patricia, became

---

7. "The Value of Education," *Think: the Magazine of Case Western Reserve University*, Cleveland, OH, Fall/Winter 2008, p. 7.

a leader in state and regional firefighting training. After his death, he was inducted into the Parma Senior High School Hall of Fame in Cleveland—this is success, by any standard. Obviously, some vocations and professions require college-level certificates and degrees. But, do not go to college simply to make more money. Having lots of money can certainly make your life very comfortable, but not always happier.

Charles J. Sykes offers fifty rules you won't learn in high school. A few of them are: "Life is not fair: Get used to it. The world won't care as much as your school does about your self-esteem. Your school might have done away with winners and losers: life hasn't. It's not your parents' fault: if you screw up, you are responsible. Be nice to nerds: you might end up working for them (we all could) Smoking does not make you look cool ... it makes you look moronic. You are not immortal." This is good advice for anyone contemplating college, as a positive and realistic attitude is a big part of being a success as a student, employee, and partner.

The above "rules" were received via e-mail from one of my coauthors of other books, and were attributed to Bill Gates, the founder of Microsoft, along with his photo, but were originated by Charles J. Sykes.[8] This offers me the opportunity to warn you to check the documentation of all Internet information as to the original source, a mandatory practice for any college student. I checked snopes.com and discovered that Bill Gates never wrote the rules and that Sykes originally wrote fourteen rules in the mid 1990's, which he expanded to fifty in his 2007 book.

While many of us acknowledge that the Internet is a fast and wonderful source of information, it can contain false data. The problem with an Internet citation is usually the lack of documentation as to the original source. One needs to check the authenticity of any e-mail. When I checked Snopes.com, I discovered that Bill

8.  Charles J. Sykes, *50 Rules Kids Won't Learn in School; Real-World Antidotes To Feel Good-Education*, New York, N.Y., St. Martin's Press, 2007. Appendix I, pp. 163–165.

Gates never wrote or stated those rules, and they were created by Charles J. Sykes. There are several versions of these rules, but I want to reinforce that the e-mail I received, quoted the wrong source and just nine rules, not fourteen.

Finally, if you cannot understand this chapter, either its vocabulary or its meaning, you are not ready for college. However, if you did "look up" a few of the more esoteric words, good for you and that's a good sign.

Okay, let's assume you are willing, able, and ready to go to college. The next question is, "What do you want to study?" Once again, those of you who have received scholarships and already know where you are going, and what you will study, might want to skip ahead to the chapters on where to live, how to succeed, and post–commencement issues.

# 2

# What Do You Want to Study?

Before deciding what school to attend, it is a good idea to have at least some idea of what you want to study or work at, or, put another way, what are some of the educational and vocational options that interest you? Notice the words "some" and "options," as you have time, within reason, to change your mind, even a short while after starting college, or leaving college. You might say, "I'm still not sure what I want to do after I grow up." I mention change because you might think you want to be a geologist, but after the first course in geology you might find that you don't like it, and that's okay. The many reentering older students are proof that you can start over within some reasonable age/time frame. In addition, what you want to study is usually the key factor in the choice of where to attend college.

Almost all high schools have a "career center" and I assume you have visited it to review the literature and references from corporations, professional societies, various government entities, trade associations, employment agencies and, of course, colleges, universities, and trade schools. Ask the counselor about current opportunities and jobs you might never have even thought about. The U.S. Government publishes a directory of all known occupations, including job descriptions, qualifications, pay, and forecasts of current and future employment—see *the Enhanced Occupational Handbook 2008–09 Edition* (or later editions), Department of Labor, Bureau of Labor Statistics, U.S. Government Printing Office, Washington, DC, or www.bls.gov/oco. If your school doesn't have a copy, visit your local library. Another good career-planning source is Discover, the ACT computer-based career information and guidance system; see *www.act.org*. But let's first expose the following popular myth, with all of its romantic nonsense:

Myth: You can do anything you want to do, if you try hard enough.

Reality: You can do some things, based on your ability or, put another way, strive to be all *you can be*, the modified U.S. Army recruiting slogan. Many experts have made this same observation, including the noted social scientist Charles A. Murray.[9] This reality obviously applies to almost all vocations. Here are a few examples that I realize all seem negative, but they will be positive for some of you who are good at chemistry, can tolerate the sight of blood, etc.:

1. You can't be a nurse or an M.D. if you can't stand the sight of blood and/or hate chemistry, or are not willing and able to master a long educational program that demands great rigor, hard work, with long hours.
2. You can't be an engineer if you hate math (or can't do it). In addition, the freshman year is brutal, probably the most demanding of all the freshman-year curriculums.
3. You can't be a lawyer if you dislike books, have a weak memory, hate to read, and/or can't present your thoughts in a logical order.
4. You can't play big-time basketball if you are 5'5".
5. You can't play football if you can't tolerate physical contact and pain.
6. You can't be in law enforcement if you are afraid of guns or bad people.

9. Charles A. Murray, *Real Education: Four Simple Truths for Bringing America's Schools Back to Reality*, New York, N.Y., Crown Forum, pp. 45–47, 2008.

7. You can't be in sales if you are stumped for an answer when someone says "Hello," and you fear rejection.
8. You can't be a playwright if you can't write, and have not had an original thought since the start of puberty.
9. You can't be a teacher if you hate kids and have little patience.
10. You can't be an airline pilot if you have chronic airsickness.
11. You can't be in the army if you are not willing to take orders.
12. You can't be in music if you are tone deaf.

This list could go on and on but I think I have made the point, which is, you must *discover* what your various aptitudes are, what you enjoy doing, and what you are good at. The two go together: we usually enjoy what we do well. An interesting guidebook is *10 Best College Majors For Your Personality*, by Laurence Shatkin, Ph.D, and the editors at JIST Publishing Co., Indianapolis, IN, 2008; www.jist.com, and *The Princeton Review 20009 Guide To College Majors*, Random House, 2009, www.princetonreview.com/bookstore. Also see *90-Minute College Major Matcher: Choose Your Best Major For a Great Career*, by Laurence Shatkin, JIST Publishing Co., Indianapolis, IN, 2007, www.jist.com. Then study and practice being the very best you can be at what you can do. Well, how do you "discover" what fits for you? Here is my list to help you find your niche:

## Discovering What You Want to Study and Do

1. The obvious first step is to review all those aptitude, personality, interest, and vocational guidance tests you have taken, the kind almost all high schools give. They reveal important clues and at least some direction, such as to

what degree you are analytical, emotional, aggressive, imaginative, science oriented, etc. ... to discover what you might do well.

2. Ask someone you know, in a vocation of your interest, what the job/profession is like. For example, ask your dentist how he/she became a dentist and what the typical day is like. If your parents work at something of interest to you, it is obvious that you have an in-home resource, although I have had students, with very little knowledge of what their parents did for a living (did they ever really talk?).

3. Read the classified ad section of your local paper and at least one national newspaper such as *The New York Times*, Sunday edition, or *USA Today*. Check Borders, Barnes and Noble, and/or your library for the national newspapers. Most classified sections run featured articles on available occupations.

4. There are now various online postings of available occupations.

5. Do not use TV shows as a guide to professions. They are way over–glamorized and fail to reveal a day-to-day routine.

6. Advanced placement (AP) college courses that are taken in high school, if available to you and you are able to do it, could be a big first taste. Taking a psychology course, at the local community college, while you are in high school, will be helpful for you to see if the subject is of special interest. Indeed, a few states, like Ohio, have special programs at selected colleges, where the state will even pay the tuition. In Ohio, the program is called the Post-Secondary Educational Opportunity Program. Check to see if your state has something similar. Advanced placement courses could also reduce the number

of college courses or credits needed for graduation—more on this subject in the "Applying" section.

7. Check the employment opportunities. As mentioned previously, while the career center data sources could help, ask those working in the field about the number of available jobs. Understand just how competitive your particular job market might be. Some, like acting, music, dance, art, paleontology, and the like, are highly competitive—many are called, but few are chosen. This does not mean you should give up your dream, but you must know the realities of just how competitive it is.

8. Remember to keep visiting the high school career and guidance center for updates, and review sources about college majors, such as those cited earlier in this chapter.

9. Visit a state unemployment office—they know job markets.

10. Seek the objective truth about your abilities, skills, talents, strengths, weaknesses, and energy level from a credible and objective source. The source could be a high school counselor, teacher, big brother/sister, uncle, aunt, family friend, etc. Just make sure they are knowledgeable, older, wiser, and willing to tell you the truth. This person might be the teacher who gave you the C, and one you do not particularly like, but one you respect. There are no perfect people in everything and that includes you, even if you have a 4.0 GPA. We cannot improve unless and until we acknowledge our weaknesses. For example, even if you have a high IQ and GPA, poor social and weak communication skills might hinder your success in college and "on the job" or, for that matter, in enjoying life.

11. Observe what kind of people work in the jobs of interest to you. What do you know about their profile, typical personality, life style, work habits, or even their social

life? Are they your kind of people? Do you want to be like *most* of them?

12. Would you be proud to be in this vocation, and are you willing to make the sacrifices to be a productive member of it?

13. Remember, many vocations have entry-progression steps involving vastly different jobs/tasks. For example, the business field of marketing, usually involves a mandatory first job that requires selling a product or service. If you think you will be starting as a manager or an analyst in strategic planning, you will be in for a shock. I taught marketing for over forty years and discovered early on that many marketing majors were terrified at the thought of being in sales, the core function. In addition, other marketing sub-functions, such as marketing research, usually require a graduate degree. Positions in advertising are often filled by English majors who can write, and art majors who are creative. Even scarier, there are many successful marketing managers—in particular, sales managers—who never went to college, but have superior persuasion, social, and communication skills.

14. The pre-professional programs—if you have decided to ultimately be a physician, a lawyer, or any other professional requiring a graduate degree or specific advanced courses, you must enroll in the necessary preparation courses. The simple way to discover what these prerequisite courses are is to ask the professional schools you plan to attend. They all have this information online or in hard copy. A word of caution: prerequisites will vary by the particular professional or graduate school, which means you must do at least some predicting of where you want to go for advanced study.

Some private, liberal art colleges have joint program agreements with graduate schools, whereby the first three years of prerequisites for engineering or medicine are done at the liberal arts colleges, and then the last two years are done at the graduate school. At the conclusion of these programs, often called a "3.2 curriculum," in the fifth year of study, the student receives both a bachelor of science degree and an engineering or medical degree. A good example of this 3.2 format is the Ohio Wesleyan University—California Institute of Technology program in engineering. These "combined" programs are popular because they are less threatening—there is less immediate academic competition, or what I call "rigor shock" in the first two years, versus direct first-year entry into engineering or even medicine. Direct entry into professional programs produces rather high failure and dropout rates. In addition, undergraduate programs usually have more merit and grant money, which results in rather substantial dollar savings. Some medical schools have early admissions programs built around the 3.2 concept.

There is also an increase in the number of joint community college and local university programs that link curriculums to allow a student to receive both an associate degree and a bachelor's degree at the end of the program. Some of these programs are called a "2.1 curriculum." There are many variations of these joint programs, but they all reduce the time and cost required to complete a four-year degree. A good example is the Midpoint Campus Center in Brunswick, Ohio, a joint venture of Lorain County Community College and the University of Akron, both in the northeastern Ohio region; visit www.midpointcampus.com.

15. One more important point: avoid being pressured by your parents, and other family members to follow in

their footsteps. You might not be able to, or want to, work at what they did or now do.

16. Mandatory "electives" beyond your major/minor Employers have told me for years, "Send me graduates (even our engineers) who are good communicators with high social skills." Regardless of your particular vocation, you need to be able to talk, write, and act/look like a college graduate/professional. These skills include "body English." Some proper speaking skills are obvious and just one error such as, "I seen," "It don't," "It ain't," etc., will kill you in an interview. We call these obvious grammar mistakes "knockout blows." Other killers include poor posture, inappropriate dress, negative facial expressions, and dumb questions, or, worse, no questions.

One of my favorite courses I taught at California State University, Fresno was called the "Psychology of Personal Persuasion." While the course title was a fancy name for personal selling, the material went well beyond the fundamentals of selling. It explored rather sophisticated communication, persuasion, and other aspects of being a good conversationalist, a skill we all need. The well-known Dale Carnegie courses cover this subject in adult classes with the slogan, "How to win friends and influence people?" See *www.dalecarnegie.com.* Unfortunately, you could graduate from college and not know how to engage in a meaningful conversation. We all must learn to be articulate, which is the skill needed to express one's self with clarity, speed, and power.

Many people fail to realize that two key conversation skills are listening and using appropriate questions in a give-and-take rhythm, called "dyadic flow." (See current books such as *The Art of Conversation: A Guided Tour of a Neglected Pleasure*, by Catherine Blyth, Gotham Books, Penguin Group, New York, 2009, and the classic work, *Getting Through to People*, by Jesse S. Niren-

19

berg, Prentice-Hall, Englewood Cliffs, NJ, 1963, revised edition, 1973, and January 1998, now out of print, but available from the used market, such as www.half.com or www.harvestbooks.com.) I'm sure you have an acquaintance who never asks you anything about what you are doing, have done, or other such questions that demonstrates a genuine interest in your activities, thoughts, and plans. Develop empathy for the other person and think of it as "us and we," versus "I and me." Seek out at least one course that will allow you to learn and practice these communication skills. In addition, these courses teach persuasion skills and how to disagree without being disagreeable. Speech departments often teach these courses, and there might be personal salesmanship and negotiation courses in the business school.

Extracurricular activities also help you to develop good social and team-building skills. Polish those social graces we call manners. Practice saying "Please," "Thank you," and "Pardon me." Whenever appropriate, I would insert in my lectures advice on when to use the various profound three-word phrases, such as: "I was wrong, I made a mistake, I am sorry, I will improve," and the real biggie, "I love you." Other etiquette rules include keeping your elbows off the table, using the correct utensils, and, for men, taking your hat off when inside. Finally, it's not only what you say, but how you say it. Smile, you will usually get one back. The old descriptions, such as "Having class" or "Being polished," seem to convey what I have been writing in this section.

As I reminded you in chapter 1, "Are You Ready?", writing skills are also critical, and as important as verbal ability. While most college courses require at least some formal written work, take as many composition courses as you can. The only way to improve your writing is to write.

As one career consultant observes, "Soft skills such as leadership, team building, organizational, and time management skills are extremely important in the workplace ... the truly successful people are the ones who make other people feel good or feel important."[10]

The table below gives ratings of desired employee candidate skills from a survey conducted by the National Association of Colleges, and Employers (college placement offices and organizations hiring college graduates), which is based on a five-point scale, with five considered extremely important and one, not important. In other words, whether you are a nurse, an engineer, a business major, or a liberal arts graduate, these are the skills employers are looking for, at least in the opinion of the National Association of Colleges and Employers:

| | |
|---|---|
| Communication Skills | 4.6 |
| Strong Work Ethic | 4.5 |
| Teamwork Skills (works well with others) | 4.5 |
| Initiative | 4.4 |
| Analytical Skills | 4.3 |
| Computer Skills | 4.3 |
| Flexibility/Adaptability | 4.3 |
| Interpersonal Skills (relates well to others) | 4.3 |
| Problem-solving Skills | 4.3 |
| Technical Skills | 4.2 |
| Detail-oriented | 4.1 |
| Organizational Skills | 4.0 |
| Self-confidence | 4.0 |
| Leadership Skills | 3.9 |
| Tactfulness | 3.8 |
| Friendly/Outgoing personality | 3.7 |
| Creativity | 3.6 |
| Strategic-planning Skills | 3.4 |

10. Terri Mrosko, "Developing Your Soft Skills," *Plain Dealer,* Cleveland, OH, May 13, 2009, Section Fl. Contact Ms. Mrosko at www.mrosko@cox.net.

Source: National Association of Colleges and Employers, reprinted from "Job Outlook, 2009," for the full report, see www.jobweb.com; with the permission of the National Association of Colleges and Employers, copyright holder.

In addition to all the skills listed above, all organizations look for good manners, including such simple things as writing thank you notes, the timely returning of telephone calls and, believe it or not, "No, sir; yes, ma'am" still works—it means you are cultured. Learn to be distinctive in a positive way; that's the real way to be "cool."

## Majors and Minors

Obviously your major is the subject you have selected to study in depth—it requires your concentration. Your major can be a single subject like history, or pre-something, as preparation for graduate work. Minors simply involve less course work in a subspecialty, and they either complement your major, such as labor economics to the economics major, or might be something different as a sort of "backup," such as a marketing minor with a major in broadcasting. I know I am biased, but marketing is a great minor for several vocations and professions, as we all have to sell ourselves and our ideas.

Okay, now you have at least some idea of what you want to do in life. This gives you direction as to what to study and where you might go to pursue your dream goal.

For some of you, if you have always known what you wanted to be, the next step is easy. For example, if you have always wanted to be an engineer, you like math; are good at it, your mother is an engineer, and you have received a full academic scholarship to

Purdue University in West Lafayette, Indiana, wow! Off you go to become a "Boilermaker."

If you are still not quite certain, generally most colleges require that the first two years include general education or what we call foundation courses in english, math, language, physical-natural science, history, social science, and even core prerequisite courses, such as economics and statistics. Thus you could and should explore a wide variety of subjects, which will help you decide what to select as a major and a minor.

Now, on to the next step: where to pursue your dream. The college you select is a very important choice because for most of you, it will be your home for four to five years and this critical experience will have a lasting impact on your entire life.

# 3

# Selecting the Right School for You: Where Do You Pursue Your Dream and How Do You Finance It?

## Selecting Your College

First, when I use only the word "school," I include colleges, universities, and other post–high school educational institutions. You will receive information and advice from your high school guidance counselors, college admissions staffs, your parents, possibly a consultant, and other mentors. Regardless of the input from others, you should work your way through this procedure, to understand the requirements. There are more options than ever before as to where to study, and they range from online to the traditional four-year college. For some of you the choice is simple. For example, let's say you want to be an X-ray technician and the local community college has a good affordable program. Bingo, what could be easier? For others, more options exist. Let's start with a list of the various types of institutions—just make sure you check their employment-placement records and accreditation status.

1. Junior or community colleges: these two-year colleges, offering certificates and associate degrees, were originally called "junior colleges." Now almost all of these as described as "public-city-community" colleges. These institutions offer certificates and

associate degrees in various technical programs, such as medical technology, nursing, law enforcement, physician's assistant, and business. They also provide core course in the basic prerequisite and remedial courses, which can lead to a four-year college degree, through transfer-of-credit agreements, called articulation agreements, with local four-year colleges. As Dr. Patricia Rowell, the western campus president of Cuyahoga Community College states, "We hope to offer everything needed for an associate's degree that can be the basis for most bachelor degrees ... Cuyahoga Community College is committed to access."[11] Access means a convenient location, low tuition and fees, rather open enrollment, and an opportunity to sample the college. While these commuter schools offer very few traditional college-life experiences, they are an excellent way for many young and reentering older students to economically experiment with college-level study, and to discover potential vocational or pre-professional interests.

Some high schools have affiliation agreements with local community colleges that allow qualified high school students to earn concurrent credits, and actually graduate with both a high school diploma and an associate degree, or at least with some college credits. These programs are also called "advanced placement" agreements with certain community colleges, and four-year institutions. Just make sure you are physically and mentally capable for this increased workload. Many college faculty members at four-year institutions question the quality of these programs, and whether high school students are mature enough for advanced study. Is it better to use the extra time in high school to engage in approved extracurricular activates, where social and team-building skills are learned? Indeed, some four-year institutions do not recognize all associate degree work from local community colleg-

11. Linda Chojinacki, "Cuyahoga Community College Unveils New Brunswick College Center," *Plain Dealer*, Cleveland, OH, October 23, 2009, p. CN1, lchojnac@plaindealer.com.

es. If you contemplate applying to a specific four-year college, be sure to check their transfer-of-credit policy and get it in writing.

2. Proprietary schools: these are private for-profit colleges, often called technical schools or institutes, and are quite common for culinary, art, music, technical, and other vocational specialties, such as auto mechanics and business. Some still use the historical descriptions of trade and/or vocational school. The *US News and World Report*'s college rating guides, call many of these institutions "schools with a specialty," such as Babson College in Boston (business) and Julliard in New York (music), because they limit their programs to one selected field. Many are tops in their field—in particular, art and music—and several are highly selective. Others are simple no-frills replicas of traditional colleges and, like all "for profits," cost more than state schools, but often have open admission, schedules to accommodate working adults, and concentrate on popular vocations such as business, medical assistants, nursing, and criminal justice. They usually require far fewer prerequisites, give credit for life experiences, and have a concentrated curriculum allowing students to complete requirements for diplomas, certificates, and degrees far faster than they would at the traditional college. A few are four-year programs and some even include graduate programs—the University of Phoenix is a classic example. Check your telephone book, yellow pages, or go online, and you will be surprised at how many of these schools are available, especially if you live in a large metro area. For many of you, the two-year associate degree is all you need to work at the vocation of your interest. Even a certificate might be sufficient. See www.petersons.com for "Peterson's Guide to Technical and Vocational Schools."

These are a few nonprofit public vocational high schools that also offer post-high school, adult education programs, in many technical fields. A few of these such as the Polaris Career Center in Middleburg Heights, Cleveland, Ohio, have credit transfer requirements with local universities. See www.polaris.edu.

You will not experience a total or typical college experience at these schools but again, you might not need or want the traditional college life of dorms, fraternities, sororities, clubs, football games, campus events, and the other out-of-class social activities.

Be careful to check for the proper accreditation and other state approvals. A few of these schools are absolute frauds, typically called, "Diploma mills." Check any airline magazine on your next flight and read the various advertisements, such as: "Earn a BA in just a few short weekends at Diploma Mill University in beautiful Carmel, no prerequisites and full credit for your work experience." Common sense should tell anybody such a promise is a gross exaggeration and no one will hire its graduates. Again, check job-placement records and accreditation status. Your high school career center's guidance counselor should be able to establish the proper accreditation for a specific program.

3. Online or in class? There are an increasing number of on-line courses and degree programs. The term "distance learning" (DL) is often used to describe courses and degree programs that use a mix of online, TV interactive lectures, and correspondence (see www.detc.org). The advantages of such offerings are somewhat obvious; the big one being that you can do most, if not all, of the study program at home, and at your convenience. They are very popular with older and reentering students attending proprietary schools. Most of these institutions have rather open admission policies with few, if any, prerequisites, test scores, and other traditional admission requirements. While such courses are adequate for the pure transmission of facts, data, methods, procedures, and other "how to do" tasks, they lack the synergy of in-class participation, the personal interaction with other students, and the instructor. For example, one can easily learn the formula to calculate the return on investment (ROI) online, but you will not learn how to sell it as a member of a financial team. In addition, there is no out-of-class learning, as mentioned in chapter 2. One cannot develop these very important social communication

27

skills "online." I only recommend an online program if that is the only way you can participate. It makes sense for older and reentry students.

Finally, the ability to offer online degree programs has produced a number of fraudulent offerings, including those using fake accreditation, usually their own inventions. One good source to check for the legitimacy of online programs is www.geteducated.com. Other traditional sources for checking credentials of all postsecondary schools are The Council of Higher Education and the United Nations (UN) Educational Scientific and Cultural Organization.[12]

4. Internships and cooperative learning opportunities: many majors and degree programs are much stronger when they include internships with working professionals. Some even require internship courses. Cooperative degree programs allow for alternating on-campus classroom study with actual employment in a vocation. These are called "co-ops," and several engineering schools incorporated this work experience requirement into their curriculum. The University of Cincinnati's School of Engineering is a good example. If these options appeal to you, investigate which institutions offer these "real-world" learning opportunities. Where appropriate, the learning value of on-the-job training is obvious. In many instances it also provides an excellent way to combine work and study as a way to finance your education.[13] This is a good example of combining "what to study" and "where to go" decisions. (See www.vault.com for information on internships and co-op programs.)

5. Private or state, small or large? Traditional private colleges are usually small liberal arts colleges, although a few are medium-

---

12. Caution Encouraged With Online Degrees, by Edith Starzyk, *Plain Dealer,* Cleveland, OH, July 5, 2009, p. A9.
13. Jones, Marcia, "Experiential Learning Gives Job Seekers and New Grads the Edge in the Market," *Plain Dealer*, Cleveland, OH, September 16, 2009, p. 1, sec. F., mjones@lorainccc.edu.

size, and some include selected graduate programs. I think the real question is the size issue. The typical private liberal arts school has around 1,200 to 2,500 students, with up to 4,000 if it is in a city, and offers some evening programs such as law and business. A student population of 8,000 or more is large for a private school, even with a full offering of professional and other graduate programs. Contrast these numbers with 30,000 to 50,000 for universities in the Big Ten, the Pac Ten, etc., and we are talking about a huge difference.

If you like and need the comfort of having only a small number of people around you, then the small, liberal arts private school is for you, but it's going to cost a lot more. Small, private-school faculty and staff members are much more caring (that is what you pay for) than the large state-school, research-focused faculty and staff. When I was a student at Michigan, we had a saying, "You have to be able to walk over bodies to survive." On the other hand, there is nothing more exciting than the buzz, excitement, and multiple events that make up large state campuses; they are alive with activities and opportunities of every nature. Like lots of decisions, it is a trade-off. What do you need more—diversity and excitement, or tender loving care?

Aside from the factors listed above and the cost differential, the large campus (state or private) offers more alternative programs in terms of curriculum, majors, and special learning opportunities. If you think you are going on to graduate school (and you must for medicine, law, a Ph.D., etc.), then for those of you who can afford it, select a small liberal arts private college with a good track record of getting its students into the better graduate schools, although the same could be said for some larger state schools. Another factor to consider, if you know for certain you are going to a specific institution for graduate work, there is the need to check with this university as to their preference for feeder undergraduate programs.

What's my personal preference? If you can afford it and/or

can obtain a scholarship, go to the good, small, private liberal arts college for its wonderful personal exposure to literature, science, and the arts. This is the basic education needed for the whole spectrum of lifelong opportunities and appreciation as well as the possibility of going on to graduate school. Having said that, I should note that there are very fine liberal arts colleges within large state universities with the obvious examples of Cal Berkeley, Michigan, and Wisconsin—if you can handle the size issue. I often think it is a question that deals with your high school experience, and did you feel "lost" if you went to a large high school? Finally, a few of you might want the all-female or all-male schools, and some still exist.

6. Liberal versus conservative. Be careful with this criterion as parents often pressure students to go where they think the school has a safe environment, "safe" meaning that the institution will reinforce a continuation of their (the parents') value system. The classic examples of very conservative, small, private colleges are Hillsdale College in Hillsdale, Michigan, and Grove City College, in Pennsylvania. Both are fine, small, private liberal arts colleges with at least some religious connections; very conservative, and probably very Republican. If this is your belief system and you can afford it, go for it. Contrast these institutions with colleges like the University of California at Berkeley, the University of Wisconsin at Madison, and Oberlin College in Oberlin, Ohio, which are very liberal, free thinking, and largely associated with Democrats. Well, take your pick as far as political flavor, if this is a major issue.

Quite frankly, most of the elite colleges and universities, and most of the faculty at all colleges (except as noted) are liberal Democrats, but unless you are a political science major, so what? Now we are back to your mom and dad. If they say they will only pay fees if you go to a *far-right college*, and you have no other choice, go to a far-right college, get your education, and then vote the way you want. This is the same advice I have often given to freshman students, "Don't run home over Thanksgiving and shock your parents with your newfound, extremely liberal thoughts—in particular, if they are paying the full bill (unless, of course, they are liberal)."

7. Religious or atheist, or somewhere in between? Few issues in life are black and white and neither is this one. Some schools have obvious, strong religious affiliations, such as Notre Dame or Holy Name, and the evangelical bible schools. Almost all of the older small liberal arts colleges were founded by religious orders, but most have reverted to rather "loose" affiliations like the colleges with Lutheran, Methodist, Congregational, Presbyterian, and Episcopal roots. These same schools have nationality origins matching their religions, with German, Norwegian, and Swedish Lutherans, along with English Episcopal and Methodist schools, being classic examples. Some of these fine, old institutions (most were founded before 1850) retain more of their heritage than others, but I doubt if any require chapel attendance. This choice depends on how much you want the institution to match your heritage, and many students want this connection to their family history. However, almost all large, state schools have religious centers of various denominations, so we always get back to the size issue.

8. Big city, or rural, or somewhere in between? I suppose the comfort zone on this issue reflects where you grew up. If you are going to school at NYU, UCLA, or USC, you must be able to cope with impersonal mobs of people and scary traffic. For many students, they like the excitement and opportunities found in big cities, while others love the charm of the very small college towns, such as Grandview, Ohio (Denison University), or medium-size towns, such as Madison (University of Wisconsin) or Ann Arbor (University of Michigan). Take your pick, but I feel the size of the town is a minor decision factor, unless you need internships and/ or work that is available only in a certain size city. If you were studying marine biology, I would think you should be by the sea

31

or a very large lake, rather than being in Des Moines, Iowa. One other thing: your social life should be on campus, not in the city, as primarily, you should *not* be in college to entertain yourself.

9. Here, or Europe, Asia, Africa, etc.? Very few of you will be faced with this choice. Unless you want to be a French teacher, or a specialist on the European Union, stay at home. Almost all colleges have "study abroad semesters" and that is what I recommend. I taught in the London Semester Program during my career at California State University Fresno and found it was a wonderful experience for both faculty and students. Graduate school seems more appropriate for overseas study, when you are more mature to handle such a dramatic change in your living environment. However, if Oxford gives you a full scholarship, grab it and go.

10. "Elite," excellent, good, average, and ... ? By "elite," at least historically, we usually mean the private Ivy League colleges. However, as the various evaluation sources listed in the appendix reveal, for what you want to study, the "elite" might be the University of California at Berkeley, the University of Michigan, in Ann Arbor, the University of Virginia, in Charlottesville, the California Institute of Technology, in Pasadena, the University of Wisconsin-Madison, Duke in Durham, North Carolina, the University of North Carolina in Chapel Hill, Penn State University in College Station, or the University of Missouri at Columbia, all of which are number one in some field, such as Missouri in Journalism. The word "elite" implies institutions which are very selective and distinguished in several fields, and this description now fits several state institutions. Moreover, even Harvard is not tops in all major fields of study. In my opinion, the "elite" colleges and universities are those listed as "most selective," and "highly selective," according to Barron's *Profiles of American Colleges* (see the appendix).

Many educators would agree that the gap in academic quality between the Ivy League and the Big Ten, the Pac Ten, Duke,

Virginia, and other very fine state research-oriented universities, has significantly narrowed. The very definition of "elite" is up for grabs, simply because we have no really objective way of measuring/defining it. Much of it is pure bias, based on history and snobbery, which might not be current—which is another way of saying the school might be living on a past reputation that is no longer valid.

The endless debate over which schools are "elite," ignores any recognition of what is the best school for you. As the distinguished educational journalist Loren Pope wrote in his best-selling book *Colleges that Save Lives: 40 Schools that Will Change the Way You Think About Colleges*, Penguin Books, New York, 2nd revised edition, 2006, there are many excellent, small private liberal arts colleges and universities to consider. The other good news about these schools is that many are more affordable and accessible than one might imagine. These are schools that focus on you, the student, with very close student-faculty collaboration, tailor-made curriculums, and they concentrate on how to think about the whole spectrum of world problems, values, and opportunities.

Learn to recognize bias as to recommendations on where to go to college. For example, if the person you are talking to in an interview, only went to a private college, it would be normal for him or her to recommend a private college; it is what they know, unless they are in the educational profession and/or are very objective. I have several friends who think you have to go to the Ivy League to get a good education, which is an obvious personal bias and defies logic. Conversely, I have some friends who believe that only public/state schools provide the "best buy" or value. Neither position is true for all students.

11. Semesters versus quarters. While I think this is a minor question, some students are concerned about the quarter system, which has more exams as well as course offerings, when compared to the semester system, which offers fewer courses, but

more depth in each one. Most schools seem to be moving to a tri-semester system.

12. Desired location after college. If you have a very strong desire to live in a certain city or area, you might want to attend a school whose alumni seem to be in charge and heavily influence hiring, appointments, and promotions. The problem with this selection factor is the lack of any objective source as to who are the actual power brokers. Just to give one example, if you told me you wanted to settle in San Francisco, I would tell you that alumni of the University of California at Berkeley are dominant in many professions and vocations. The problem is, I can't prove this personal opinion. This location issue might be far more important as to where you want to go after graduate school—in particular, for law, business, and medicine.

This seems to be a good point at which to talk about the link between motivation and getting a good college education. I suspect the typical college is not very demanding. Combine this observation with my earlier comments regarding easy grading, and one can conclude that the typical college student, at the average college, will not be seriously challenged, academically. This, lack of rigor, and lack of a highly competitive class environment means you can probably get by with nominal effort, especially in classes taught by instructors with low academic standards or who fail to require attendance. We always get back to the question of how badly do *you* want to learn a particular subject and, "Are you ready for college?" Even if you are not challenged, you can maximize the value you receive from any course, at any school. Perhaps the real lesson is, you do not need to go to an "elite" school to get a sound education, but in the future, the reputation of the better schools will open up more doors to vocational opportunities and/or graduate schools. If you have the ability and funds, try to attend an elite institution.

Again, seek advice on college selection from an objective, knowledgeable source. The data sources in the appendix will help, but the final choice must be what you feel meets your educational needs. All schools are victims of the "rumor mills," which means individuals with limited or no real experience at the institution spread highly inaccurate and exaggerated assertions about the particular campus. Get the facts and responsible opinions, and ignore the wild stories.

Finally, pick the school that fits you, your study plan and, if possible, your parents' recommendations. But for heaven's sake, don't have a nervous breakdown because Princeton turned you down, or bankrupt yourself or your family to attend one of the very expensive schools. If you want one of the "elite" colleges and get a full scholarship to one, obviously grab it and go. If not, there are many other excellent universities for you to attend, so explore the options and remember that even the so-called elite colleges and universities might not offer what you want to study, and/or you might not feel they fit your comfort zone. Resist being pressured into attending where your mom, dad, or another relative went, unless it coincides with your own choice. Again, never blindly follow your high school friends; there are lots of interesting people to meet at college appropriate for your study needs and future.

## Making the Decision, "Where Do I Go?"

The appendix (part A) to this chapter lists most of the major rating/evaluation guides available in your high school career room, library, online, in the local library, or you can buy most of them at Borders, Barnes & Noble, or Amazon.com. In addition, make sure you ascertain whether the schools you are interested in are accredited by an appropriate agency, such as The Higher learning Commission of the North Central Association of Colleges, and Secondary Schools, and other regional associations. These associations determine a school's adequacy of libraries, financial stability, facilities, student turnover, reputation, degree requirements, qualifications of faculty, and other such standards, including entrance requirements and curriculum adequacy. Their basic objective is to certify/verify that the schools are legitimate (that they are what they claim) and meet minimum requirements.[14] However, they seldom rank schools by quality ratings. Many states also require a type of license. Beware of somewhat phony accrediting statements that imply accreditation when in fact the college is not so recognized. There are also special accreditations for specific disciplines, such as those provided by the Association to Advance Collegiate Schools of Business (AACSB), the American Bar Association (ABA) for law schools, and various scientific, medical, and other professional societies.

Regarding diversity in student enrollment, while all schools have greatly expanded their mix of students by race, gender, nationality, religion, cultural and financial background, you will meet a more diverse group at the typical community college and/ or state university than at a smaller private college. You can indeed learn much from "different" people, especially in this global world.

I suggest you start a folder for each possible institution you are interested in. In each folder place:

1. Brochures and application forms from the school. Visit them on any local "college fairs/nights" held by high schools and local colleges to collect data or obtain them from websites or by mail. If you are still unsure as to what schools you might want to apply, try using the College Navigator at www.nces.ed.gov/collegenavigator.

2. A copy of their website information. What are they emphasizing?

3. Notes you have taken from your interviews with graduates

---

14. For an interesting example, see "The Jack Welch MBA Coming to Web," by Paul Glader, *The Wall Street Journal*, June 22, 2009, pp. B1–2.

of the institution, employers who hire its graduates, and current students you might know.

4. Your visit experience. If possible, visit the campus, include an official tour with a designated guide from admissions, and then wander around on your own and get a feel for the place. What is the atmosphere, how does it look, feel, and smell? Talk to students and ask them how they like or don't like the college, get both the good and bad points, as there is no perfect place. Based upon your interest, try to attend a college event such as a play or a music concert. Explore the halls, classrooms, museums, library, labs, dorms, student center/union, and some typical campus entertainment/food centers. Read the bulletin boards and kiosks, walk around the campus, and try to catch the flavor/personality, feel the warmth, the tenor, history, and ambiance; the total feeling of this college. Grab a copy of the student newspaper and read the editorials. You might be able to experience an overnight visit in a dorm. Check to see what clubs and student organizations are available. Use your digital camera and take photos. Be sure to take notes and place them, along with candid photos, in your folder. Ask yourself, "Do I want to be a part of this academic community? Do I fit in with what I see and feel? Can I strive to be all I can be in this setting?" In short, does this place turn you on and motivate you to join this institution where you will live, work, study, and play for at least four years? Many students make several visits if the institutions are reasonably close. Do not be afraid to go back "one more time."

If you can, try to talk to a professor in the major that interests you. Ask specific questions regarding class size and how his or her class is conducted. Even a small college will have at least some larger classes, but what is the average class size in your major? All schools have at least a few large lecture sessions with smaller post-lecture discussion groups. Ask for a sample syllabus from the fundamental course as this will tell you the mechanics of a specific course.

If you are at a large research-oriented university, find out how many courses are taught by teaching assistants (TAs) versus professors. TAs are Ph.D. candidates and, like all teachers, some are excellent, good, average, and poor. If any are foreign nationals with English as a second language, can you understand them? Ask the students about the quality of teaching—in particular, are the TAs understandable?

5. History/age: there is significant merit in the concept that institutions that have survived for a long time must be doing something right. A long heritage means the cultural foundations are usually strong, along with the obvious asset accumulation, in terms of philosophy, facilities, alumni base, endowment, and reputation of quality. Traditions come with age and much of college life is about experiencing tradition.

6. Articles, newspaper stories, and other information sources. Anything that can add to your evaluation should be in the folder, and I even suggest clipping a college's advertisment in magazines and newspapers. Try to view their TV commercials, which are usually shown during sporting events. I am amazed that some college presidents are now on TV, pitching their schools. Hardly the image of dignity, but I guess somebody thinks it is good marketing.

7. Transfer-of-credit policy: this point is very important if you know you might transfer from a proprietary school or a two-year community college. Check the willingness of the four-year school to accept credits from other institutions. For that matter, this question might apply to any school you might attend, as you never know if you might transfer from one school to another. Also, get the policy in writing, just as you should for other critical facts such as tuition, fees, and refund policy.

8. Financial stability: the economic recession of 2008–2009 has made this criterion even more important, for both state and private schools. Institutions with weak finances and inadequate endowments tend to engage in many cost-cutting survival tech-

niques such as deferred maintenance, reduced class offerings, and even the elimination of majors and minors you might want, as well as other student services. Deferred maintenance can result in poor living, classroom, and laboratory environment. Check the history of such actions; ask to see the financial reports. Has summer school ever been canceled? Proprietary or for-profit technical schools could suddenly close as they are for-profit businesses and refunds could be difficult to obtain.[15]

9. Making the decision: you should now be ready to make an educated decision. Some of you might want to set up a spreadsheet matrix on your computer, with the institution in the left vertical list and characteristics/criteria variables in the horizontal columns. If you haven't decided on the type of institution (large, state, private, small, etc.), then you will need to construct several spreadsheets, one for each type of school so that you compare "apples to apples." In other words, do not compare MIT to Oberlin as they are vastly different institutions. Select your own rating scale—say, 1–10, with 1 meaning they don't have what you want, and 10 meaning "excellent." You might also want to write an essay listing advantages and disadvantages of each school. The following table will give you some idea of this common method of organizing and analyzing data. Most college instructors use spreadsheets and so will you. The following is a sample spreadsheet for analyzing college selection for undergraduate, international business-school programs, using school ratings from the *2009 Edition of America's Best Colleges*, published by *US News and World Report*, www. usnews.com, p. 120 of the printed version.

---

15. Janet Okoben, "Computer Training School's Closing May Cost Students." *Plain Dealer,* Cleveland, OH, January 6, 2010, pp. B1 and B3.

| | Criteria Variables | | | | | | | | | | | | |
|---|---|---|---|---|---|---|---|---|---|---|---|---|---|
| Institution | Curriculum | Size | Location | Facilities | Atmosphere | Faculty | Reputation/ Ranking | Job Placement | Graduate School Acceptance | Financial Stability | Scholarship Possibility | Cost | Notes |
| University of S. Carolina—Columbia (Moore) | | | | | | | | | | | | | |
| Univ. of Pennsylvania (Wharton) | | | | | | | | | | | | | |
| New York University (Stern) | | | | | | | | | | | | | |
| Univ. of Michigan—Ann Arbor | | | | | | | | | | | | | |
| Univ. of Southern California (Marshall) | | | | | | | | | | | | | |
| Univ. Texas—Austin (McCombs) | | | | | | | | | | | | | |
| List other schools of interest below | | | | | | | | | | | | | |
| | | | | | | | | | | | | | |

The names in brackets indicate the individuals who endowed the schools. USC and Texas tied for fifth. This is just one example and you might want to change the criteria variables, and of course select the institution based on what you want to study or by type of institution. It would be interesting to keep checking later editions of the annual ranking by *US News* to see if the rankings have changed, and if they do, check as to the reasons.

Working your way through this decision process is the key to learning which schools are appropriate for what you need and want. Finally, list your choices in order: 1, 2, 3, 4... to possibly eight, as you might not be admitted to, or receive a scholarship to, your first choice. For some of you, the selection is simple, because you have already received acceptance to the school of your choice.

10. Completing the application process: my favorite guidebook for this critical step is *Get Into College,* by Rachel Korn, and Jennifer Yetwin Kabat, special editors of Hundreds of Heads Books, Atlanta, GA, 2009. (See the appendix to this chapter, Part A, for other sources.) If you or your parents are totally confused by this procedure, you might want to hire a professional college advisor and, as previously advised in chapter 1, make sure he or she is certified with the CCPS designation and is a member of HECA and/or IECA.

Using one of the sources listed in part A of the appendix to this chapter, surf the web as all colleges and universities have websites that contain deadline dates for submission of application forms, requests for financial aid, essays, recommendation letters, transcripts, biographies, and other required information. Many institutions have multiple deadlines for different data, so be careful. You might already have this information in brochures you received in the mail, or obtained during visits, or from your high school career center. Make sure you have current information.

I have previously noted that most experts suggest applying to six to eight schools, even if you have been selected for admission

41

by your first choice, as you have nothing to lose by shopping for a better financial package, or a more appealing educational experience/opportunity. Potential student athletes should remember that letters of interest are not NCAA-approved formal letters of intent awards, and your coach cannot complete your application form for you. A good Internet source for application information is www.collegeboard.com.

Almost all counselors and admission staffs list the following criteria for determining acceptance by the institution. The list is almost universal, but with the exception of grades, class rank, and test scores, the weights given per item vary with each college or university, and they might change from year to year. The admissions staff of each institution has determined their desired entering-class profile, or composition according to various demographics such as sex, age, ethnic background (or diversity), city, state, country of the applicant's high school, SAT/ACT scores, talent/skill sets, majors, disadvantaged status, and other varied factors. Some have quotas for minority students and the definition of "minority" can vary by the particular school.

Here is my list of these universal criteria, as I see it, in order of importance:

1. Grade point average (GPA): all schools start with this one, but vary in the way they dissect the GPA into grades in specific courses that they regard as rigorous and indicator courses for specific majors. For premed students, they review grades in chemistry, biology, and other sciences; for engineering, math and physics; for English, literature and composition; and other obvious preparation courses for specific majors. The admissions staff are looking for high grades in what is commonly described as the college prep track. Many also give weight to the academic reputation of the high school, which is called

the "High School Profile," and your high school has this information.

2. Class rank: this factor is always a key one.
3. ACT/SAT Scores: 36 is a perfect combined ACT score and 2400 is a perfect combined SAT score. Good scores are the average test scores of the students in the schools where you are applying. Take one of the many preparation courses, such as Kaplan, for each test. If you have not scored well on these tests (you can take them several times), there is still hope when you excel in the other factors, and how you fit into their desired class profile. Many college professors feel there is too much emphasis on test scores, to the exclusion of the other very important criteria. We all know there are many very capable and high achievement college graduates who did not test well.
4. Essays: I rate this factor rather high because in highly selective schools, where the first round of elimination involves academics, the essay is often the deciding factor. In fact, more and more schools are placing increasing weight on the quality of the essay. After all, if you can't write or express yourself, how on earth are you going to succeed in college? Essays could and often do break the ties. *Get Into College*, by Jay Brody, has an excellent special section on writing essays. Also, see *College Essays That Made a Difference*, 3rd ed. by the staff at the Princeton Review, New York, Random House, 2008, www.princetonreview.com.
5. Extracurricular activities: all schools look for leadership, extra effort, civic contributions, willingness to compete, and other indicators of social skills. Also: service in student government, participation in special-interest clubs, in sports, music, drama, speech, art, dance, and community service. These and other "extras" are very

important plus points. Whenever you do something you do not have to do, it tells the person reviewing your application that you are more competitive and have more energy than those who simply do what they have to do.

6. Achievements and special recognition: this is part of the extracurricular activities record but now highlights specific honors and awards you have received. Some are obvious, such as being the class valedictorian or salutatorian. Other honors include being the class commencement speaker, a member of the honor society, a winner of the speech contest; being an Eagle Scout; selection to the all-city football team, or to the all-state girls' basketball team; being a member of an award-winning band; election as president of the Thespian Society; being the student council president, or a winner of the modern dance contest, etc. These achievements are also used to award merit scholarships and grants.

7. Personal interviews: unfortunately, most of you will not have a personal interview due to time limitations. This is another reason the essay is so important. This same limitation applies to the admission's staff in regard to their ability to interview your teachers, coaches, and advisors. If you do have the opportunity to interview, review my interview guides listed in chapter 7.

8. Written teacher, coach, and advisor recommendations: be careful in asking these mentors for recommendations, and by caution, I mean, do not assume they will write what you want; a positive endorsement. Ask only those who really know you in the subject of the particular recommendation. Discuss your request with them, in some detail—do not simply e-mail your request to the potential reviewer.

9. Special diversity goals of the college: as previously mentioned, this is part of profiling the entering freshman

class. It might involve an actual quota for members of a specific minority, a disadvantaged group, or other special groups, such as Native Americans. Many of these admission goals also have attached financial-aid packages. It could also include recruiting more students who want to major in science, or who have higher ACT/SAT scores, or are in the top 5 percent of their high school class, and many other areas. A few schools have even sought more males if they become worried about the balance of females and males.

10. The "X" factor: I call this the composite evaluation of the preceding nine factors plus the "gut" feeling of the intangibles, which might simply be the perception of the admissions office as to whether the applicant fits in. While inherently subjective, this is the reality of the final judgment of whether you are in, out, or on hold. Perhaps the best definition of what I call the "X" factor is given by William R. Fitzsimmons, the Dean of Admissions and Financial Aid at Harvard, who recently stated, "What we tend to look for more than ever are character and personal qualities."[16]

It is more important to note that these same ten factors are often used to award merit scholarships and even need-based financial assistance.

Again, watch those deadlines, as there are several different ones including the one of the initial application, the final reporting of grades (transcripts), reports of class standing, test scores, and a deadline for requests for financial aid. The typical drop-dead application date is May 1 of your senior year. This means that you must start the final application process at the start of your senior

16. *Get Into College*, by Rachel Korn and Jennifer Yetwin Kabat, special editors of Hundreds of Heads Books, Atlanta, GA, 2009, p. 174

year. For financial aid, deadlines vary as to the particular school and state. Link onto the school's website to find the "Priority filing deadline for entering freshmen." There will be more information on financing in the next section. One more warning—never pay anybody to complete your application forms and/or for the promise to "get you into any school." While you will need advice as to how to complete the paperwork, only you can do it, and it is part of the learning process. Even more important, only the admission's staff of a particular school could admit you to their institution.

Never assume it is hopeless to get into an elite college or university. Ignore all your fears and apprehensions that you will never be accepted. Ignore all those rumors that unless you score very high on the ACT or the SAT, you will never get in. As I have discussed, schools use a variety of decision factors concerning admitting or not admitting you and it is the total assessment—the "X" factor—that counts. You will learn something from each application you complete, you can't get in if you don't try, and you can apply several times to any particular school.

An experienced high school counselor, Mrs. Julia Williams, offers the following sound advice:

1. Listen and take notes from all those advising you.
2. There is a great deal of data on websites. Take advantage of the many sources of information.
3. Do not wait until December of your senior year to take the SAT and ACT tests. As early as possible (no later than your junior year), take the prep or PSAT and the PLAN, the prep test for the ACT; yes, you can take these tests many times. Full preparation courses, such as those taught by Kaplan, are very valuable.
4. Have a Plan B or other alternatives in case your first choice does not work out.
5. Many colleges and universities, even community col-

leges, require placement tests, depending upon your GPA and test scores. These placement tests indicate if you need remedial courses.

6. Only you can complete applications. "While you could get help," she says, "the coach will not fill it out for you."

7. "Attitude is more important than aptitude." She is talking about the drive and willingness to keep trying. It is not uncommon for a student to reapply several times to a school of choice—don't give up early in the process.[17]

One final bit of advice—as any academic counselor will tell you, do not blindly follow your high school friends to the same college. If you need this kind of security, you are probably not ready for college. The longer you live, the more you will realize that there are many, many potential friends and partners.

## Financing Your Education—Debt Management

For openers, the vast majority of college students work their way through school by a combination of scholarships, federal/state aid, loans, work study, waiting tables in dorms, fraternities and sororities in exchange for food, and some assistance from parents/relatives. Very few have ever had the luxury of their mom and dad or "Uncle Charlie" paying all the bills. This ranks right up there with the fact that most college students are, have been, and always will be the first in their family to go to college. From my forty-five-plus years of experience, I can safely say, if you want it

---

17. From a personal interview with Mrs. Williams of Strongsville High School, Strongsville, OH, December 16, 2009. Strongsville High School has approximately 2,500 students with 596 in the senior class. This comprehensive four-year high school is located in a large suburb of Cleveland, and has been rated "excellent" for eight consecutive years by the Ohio Department of Education.

bad enough, you can find a way to pay for it. It might take you a long time and one or two "stops and starts," but while college is even more expensive than before, there are also more financing/scholarship opportunities than ever before, and one more time—you can still work your way through. I have had many students do just that, as I did at the University of Michigan.

All colleges have financial assistance personnel, so use them. There are several sources listed in the appendix. My favorite scholarship, if you can earn one, is the military ROTC Program, which actually pays you a stipend, and provides an instantaneous professional job upon graduation, in addition to earning you financial assistance for graduate school. Of course, you have to be both physically and mentally fit, plus be prepared to take and give orders, which might be unacceptable for many of you.

You might want to sample college, at a low cost, by attending a local community college while living at home. See if you like it by going part-time and working full-time. Start a savings account to build up your education fund. For others, joining the military is a great way to gain maturity, learn technical skills (it's not all street fighting in Afghanistan), and banking reenlistment bonuses, while earning educational credits and payments for college after you leave the service.

Part B of the appendix to this chapter lists several sources of how to finance your education. You should review at least two and you or your parents might want to employ a professional consultant, as mentioned in the application section of this chapter. There are many tax issues to be considered, including income shifting, special deductions, and various state tax rules. The consultants could run various models to determine the "best buy." Many of these consultants are also financial planners and CPAs, an obvious advantage. Again, make sure they are accredited and members of IECA, HECA, or both, and not simply trying to sell you an instant plan, insurance, a promise to "get you in" to a particular school or charge you to find a scholarship. Finally, obtain a copy of IRS

Publication 970, "Tax Benefits for Higher Education." See www.
irs.gov/forms pubs/pubs.html or phone 1-800-tax-form.

High school and college advisors could also render financial advice at no charge, and the college counselors know much more than the consultants about the special scholarships and assistance opportunities at their school. Remember, lots of private scholarships are based on need, service to the school, affiliation with specific organizations such as religious orders, and national service organizations, and are not based solely on high grades and/or specific skills.

Of course, if you have a particular superior skill or affiliation, such as those listed in the criteria for admission in the previous section, check to see if the school has a scholarship or grant for you. Just remember, high-activity scholarships in areas such as music, drama, and athletics are wonderful, but you will earn them with hours of practice and performance. You cannot be a party animal and also successfully compete in these time-consuming activities. Again, your high school counselor could also advise you and your parents, regarding scholarships—in particular, for Federal student aid. Finally, lots of students use the summer to bankroll for a large part of the fall and winter semesters. Some (this author included) waited tables at dorms, fraternities, and sororities in return for food, and we even ate better than most other students.

The first step is to attend your high school guidance counselor session/briefing on financial considerations. Among other recommendations, you will be told to complete the Free Application for Federal Student Aid (FAFSA). See: ww.fafsa.ed.gov. Note the word "free" and it means just that—never pay anybody to submit this application for you. There are several unscrupulous individuals who are selling fraudulent student aid services. There are three phases to the FAFSA process: before beginning the FAFSA, filling out the FAFSA, and the FAFSA follow-up. The website will explain each of these stages, the federal and state financial aid deadlines, and will display the worksheets that tell you what data are needed. Almost any counselor and the U.S. Department of Education will tell you to adhere to the following advice, which is on the FAFSA website, with these slight additions by me:

1. Carefully read the instructions and make sure you understand the terms.
2. Apply early. State and school deadlines will vary and tend to be early, and financial aid deadlines are usually different than application deadlines.
3. Complete your tax return (you and your parents, if you are still a dependent). Do this *before* filling out your FAFSA.
4. Save time: file electronically online.
5. While many schools and states accept the FAFSA as the only required document, some do not. Ask if any additional forms are needed.
6. Complete the FAFSA, even if you think you and your family do not need financial help. You never know if your financial situation will change. Witness the thousands of students who had to quit college during the financial crisis of 2008–2009. In addition, the FAFSA is often used for other purposes such as a support document for scholarships and grants, not tied to financial aid or "need."
7. Need-based aid is calculated from the data in the FAFSA, which is used by all schools. Approximately 200 "elite" schools also use the College Board Profile. Both forms are completed online.
8. You must complete an FAFSA each year.
9. Why fill out an FAFSA? The FAFSA is the first step in applying for Federal student financial aid, such as the Pell Grant; student loans such as the Stanford, Perkins, and PLUS Federal Loans; college work-study; and state

and individual college financial aid. Remember, your government financial aid will be paid to you through the school. It will pay tuition, fees, and room and board (if provided) with the remaining balance given to you for other expenses.

After your FAFSA is reviewed, you will receive a "Student Aid Report" (SAR) by e-mail or post. If you are a dependent, the return address should be that of your parent or other legal guardian. In the upper right of the SAR front page, you will find the 'expected family contribution,' or EFC. The schools you have selected to receive SARs now use the EFC to prepare a financial aid package (grants, loans, and/or work-study), which is the difference between your EFC and the school's cost of attendance, or COA. The COA includes tuition, fees, room and board, books, supplies, cost of a computer and other required equipment, transportation to and from the college (one round trip per semester), and personal expenses. Each school must have a COA, but just make sure it is the total COA and not a promotional figure, often used in their marketing programs, which might not have all the cost factors added in.

We now have your "financial need," which is COA minus EFC. This need dollar amount is paid for or provided from a combination or package of free grants, state and federal aid, student loans, and work-study. By the way, work-study is subject to taxes. It should now be apparent that your financial aid will vary considerably by institution and state. Furthermore, either you or your parents have to think in terms of after-tax dollars. Some useful websites for student aid information are www.studentaid.ed.gov and www.students.gov.

Another important source of support money is based on merit and affiliation with various organizations, ethnic groups, special foundations, and your local community. We typically call this form of assistance scholarships, grants, or tuition waivers. I introduced many of these programs in the application criteria section of this chapter. Always check to see if the schools where you are applying have special scholarships for your particular skill, talent, field of study, heritage or membership group. Many of these scholarships and grants are available, regardless of need. While I was teaching at California State University, Fresno, the Smittcamp family established the Smittcamp Family Honors College Full-ride Scholarship, an academic scholarship based on a combination of merit, need, and community involvement. It pays for almost all expenses. Two good, free online scholarship-grant databases are: Fastweb, www.fastweb.com and Mach 24, www.collegenet.com. The school's websites also list their own unique merit scholarships. Do not forget to ask what might be available for your specific situation, as there are many unusual scholarships. One of my scholarships at Michigan offered funds to students who had a direct relative who had served in World War I. Lucky for me my father had indeed served in World World I. I also received a very low interest loan from the Knights Templar, a Masonic order.

10. Never assume that a particular school is too expensive for your budget. The real cost of attending is what's left after deductions for financial aid that is based on need, merit scholarships, and tuition waivers. For example, the 2008–09 expenses (COA) at Colgate University, a top private school in Hamilton, NY, were $39,545, but 34 percent of the undergraduates received an average aid package of $34,659. Thus, the actual cost to these students qualified for financial aid was $4,886; much less

than most state universities.[18] Indeed, many elite schools offer tuition-free attendance, based on many different factors.

11. "Don't Get Scammed On Your Way to College" is the very appropriate title of a U.S. Department of Education flyer (2004–06, v. 1). Here is their warning list:

    a. "This scholarship is guaranteed or your money back." Get refund policies in writing.

    b. "You can't get this information anywhere else." Almost all data relating to the college application and financial aid process are available free on multiple websites.

    c. "May I have your credit card or bank account number to hold this scholarship?" Usually this is an obvious scam to drain your account. Do not give any such information to anybody but verified school officials *and never on the phone.*

    d. "We'll do all the work." As I have said before, only you can apply for admission, scholarships, grants, and other financial aid.

    e. "The scholarship will cost you some money." This is pure nonsense; "free money" doesn't cost anything.

    f. "You've been selected by a national foundation to receive a scholarship" or "You're a finalist in a contest" (that you did not enter). This is usually from somebody imitating a legitimate foundation, federal agency, or corporation.

    g. I'm adding the following to the above list: "For a fee, I can get you into 'X' college." It is worth repeating that only the official admissions staff of a college or university can "get you in." For more in-

---

18. US News and World Report, 2009 Edition: "America's Best Colleges," Washington, DC, 2008, p. 217, www.usnews.com/store

formation and to report scams, visit: www.ftc.gov/ schoalrshipscams, or telephone the national fraud information center at 1-877-382-4357 (the Federal Trade Commission).

This section is merely an introduction to financing your education. See the sources I have listed in the appendix, part B, for a detailed investigation. It should now be evident that "shopping" at six to eight schools is prudent, and that there are lots of "free" dollars out there. As I have mentioned several times in this book, most college students receive some kind of financial assistance. The more you contribute and earn, the more important the college experience will be for you. When it's your dollars paying for class, the greater the incentive to attend class and learn. I call it "earning and learning," or buying into your education, the key to a successful future.

One last factor to consider is the refund policy of the particular institution you are considering. In particular, some for-profit colleges make it difficult to withdraw and/or to obtain a refund. While almost all schools must allow withdrawals, you might be charged a portion of the fees and tuition, depending upon how soon you decide to quit.[19]

---

19. Sheryl Harris, "For-Profit Schools Must Let You Quit," *The Plain Dealer,* Cleveland, November 8, 2009, pp. D1. Also, see the U.S. Government Accountability Report, September 2009 (www.gao.gov). In addition, check to see if your area has financial assistance information available, such as the non-profit Cleveland Scholarship Program Resource Center. sherylharris@plaind.com.

# How Long Will It Take?

One more cost factor is the number of semesters, quarters, or total years the typical student will require to obtain his or her degree at a particular institution, for a specific major. There are many factors affecting the length of time, including: changing majors, which usually adds prerequisites as well as more core courses; transferring to another college; required remedial courses; the number of times specific courses are offered; students dropping out for a quarter or a semester to work; illness or other "personal" reasons; the availability and utilization of summer courses; the number of hours taken per semester, or per quarter; the requirement to repeat courses; and other unexpected reasons. While the normal time taken to obtain a bachelor's is four years, I know of at least one recent case where an individual took seven years to obtain her B.S. degree in nursing, to work her way to a great career, and in her words, it was "time well invested."

Ask the college admission's counselors for the appropriate statistics and plan accordingly. Just because someone tells you that he or she took five years to finish, it doesn't always mean it cost him or her more as they might have simply taken a year off to work. However, be sure to check as to the availability of classes you need. Are they offered every semester, in the summer, during a compressed winter semester, and are there other options? Some schools have reduced the number of class sections and courses, due to financial problems. Ask to review class schedules for the past few years, and predictions for the future.

In a recent study (2009) by the American Enterprise Institute, the researchers found that fewer than 60 percent of new students graduated from four-year colleges within six years. As one might expect, the completion rates were far lower for the non- and less-competitive schools. While America's most competitive and highly competitive institutions, based on admissions selectivity rates as listed in Barron's *Profiles of American Colleges*, often

55

dominate popular discussions about quality, the vast majority of the nation's colleges and universities are less selective, and more students attend these schools.[20] While the study does not give reasons for their findings, the authors do acknowledge that the statistics fail to account for transfers. I have already mentioned such factors as transfers, voluntary dropout, flunking out, skipping terms, reduced academic credit loads, and non-availability of required courses, as reasons for low graduation rates and extended time to complete the normal four-year degrees. Check the study for the rates of the 1,385 colleges listed, and always ask for such documentation from the specific colleges you are considering.

Now that you know which college, you have another major decision to make. "Where do I live?" The choice plays a very important factor in whether you succeed or not. It is the subject of the next chapter.

---

20. Frederick M. Hess, Mark Schneider, Kevin Carey, and Andrew P. Kelly, *Diplomas and Dropouts: Which Colleges Actually Graduate Their Students (and Which Don't)*, Washington, D.C. American Enterprise Institute, p. 6, June, 2009. www.aei.org. Also, see *The Lowering of Higher Education in America*, by Jackson Toby, op cit. pp. 89–95.

# Appendix: Sources for College Profiles, Evaluations, Ratings, Scholarships, and Financing

Before you read any of the following data sources, here are a few pointers to help you make sense out of all this varied data. By the way, always check for the latest edition, as most are revised yearly. However, institutions rarely change much over just a few years, so a fairly recent edition will probably still be useful.

1. Think in terms of what is a "best buy," to use the Consumers Union term. What might be a good school for you academically, might not be a "good buy" if it costs too much for your budget.
2. How many schools should you apply to? The answer is, "It depends," as there are many variables to consider, including all the factors we have discussed in the first three chapters. If you are eligible for several scholarships at schools that appeal to you, then shop for the best total assistance package. The Independent Educational Consultants Association (IECA) survey reveals that most counselors suggest applying to six or seven schools.[21] I think your high school counselor is the best individual to help you decide on the number of applications to submit.
3. There will be several choices for you, which means you

---

21. *Get Into College*, Rachel Korn, and Jennifer Yetwin Kabat, special editors, Hundreds of Heads Books, LLC, Atlanta, GA, 2009. p. 138.

should avoid making a premature decision, on just one school.

4. Watch for the application deadline dates. Start the selection process early to avoid being forced into a panic decision at the last minute. Apply to several possible schools, as discussed in number 2. In particular, find out the deadlines for financial assistance. Generally, you must apply for admission and financial aid one year prior to attending a particular institution.

5. Usually, the best advice is to go where you have the best scholarship/assistance package, with "other things being somewhat equal." Obviously, do not simply take the money from a school that does not fit what you need and want; base your decision on factors discussed earlier in this chapter. Also, see the various reference books listed in the appendix.

6. Use at least two sources to compare ratings.

7. Make sure you compare similar evaluations and profiles; i.e., compare apples to apples. For example, you will notice some rating sources divide the school categories into national, regional, private, public, small liberal arts, graduate, etc. If you have already decided on going to a small liberal arts college, then do not compare Ohio State University to Ohio Wesleyan University. However, you will note that for some disciplines, such as international business, the top schools are large institutions.

8. Always remember, what might be the number one school in the discipline you want to study, might not be the right place for you based on earlier comments I made in this chapter, or because you can't afford it.

9. Warning: the further away from home potential colleges are, the higher the travel expenses for you and your family. Factor these costs into your budget. In addition, long distances might mean you can't make quick trips home

for short holidays like Thanksgiving. The good news about long travel time: you can't easily run home and give up, nor can your parents continue to "mother you," at every challenge.

10. If you have received an appointment to one of the U.S. Military service academies, good for you, take it. These are superior institutions and even after your military career, employers seek alumni from these academies, if only because they know how rigorous they are in *selecting* students and how tough/*competitive* it is, both physically and mentally, to survive their degree programs. In addition, they are free (a value of at least $400,000) and you have an automatic professional job after graduation.

11. SAT/ACT: I'm sure your high school career center has ample material on these tests and how to prepare for them, including available preparation courses. The following "Selected Guides" also contain source books which include information on SAT and ACT test taking. For the ACT, visit www.actstudent.org; for the SAT, visit www.collegeboard.com.

12. Finally, remember, while evaluation/rating sources help and their student profiles are indeed useful, they are subjective, as they have to be. We do not have an objective national college rating system. Make sure you read the methods used by these sources to compile their data.

## Selected Guides to U.S. Colleges and Universities

Most of the following sources are available or can be ordered at Borders, Barnes & Noble, Amazon.com, other large bookstores, at public libraries, and your high school career center. While several of the works cited below contain advice on taking SAT and ACT tests, there are many other sources on how to take these college entrance exams, and where to find prep courses. Most high school counseling centers have them. If not, visit your local library or bookstore. Just remember, rating guides are just a starting point, and you should consider all of the other criteria discussed in this chapter.[22]

Part A: General Profiles and Guides

1. *US News and World Report*'s Ultimate College Guide, 2009, ed., Sourcebooks, Inc., Naperville, IL, 630-961-3900. Note: *US News* also publishes yearly editions in the form of special issues; see www.usnews.com/store.
2. *2009 Barron's Profiles of American Colleges, 28th ed. 2008*, with CD-ROM edition by the College Division of Barron's Educational Series, Hauppauge, NY, www. barronseduc.com.
3. *Newsweek/Kaplan How To Get Into College, 2009*. Admissions guides, SAT & ACT examples, data on financial aid, the 12 top rivalries in America, and profiles of *Newsweek*'s "350 Most Interesting Schools." *Newsweek*, New York, N.Y. 2008, 866-741-0122, www.newsweek. com.
4. *The Princeton Review: Complete Book of Colleges*: up-to-date information on 1,821 colleges and universities, 2009 ed., Random House, New York, 2009 ed., www. princetonreview.com., 800-273-8439. Also, *The Princeton Review 2009 Guide to College Majors*.
5. *College Board College Handbook, 2009*, by the College Board, New York, NY. Information on 2,100 four-year and 1,700 two-year colleges, 212-713-8000, www.

22. Janet Okoben, "Those Popular Rankings of Colleges—Only a Starting Point, Counselors Say," *The Plain Dealer*, Cleveland, OH, August 20, 2009, pp. 1A and A6, jokoben@plaind.com.

collegeboard.com and *College Board Book of Majors, 2009.*

6. *Fiske Guide to Colleges, 2009* (since 1982), by Edward B. Fiske, Sourcebooks, Inc. Naperville, IL www.sourcebookscollege.com.

7. *Big Book of Colleges, 2009*, College Prowler, edited by Amy Campbell, Matt Hamman, Bridget Joyce, and Jen Vella. Pittsburgh, PA, 2008, www.collegeprowler.com.

8. *Kaplan College Guide 2009: Profiles of More Than 390 Colleges and 35 Fields*, Kaplan Publishing, New York, NY 2009, www.kaplanpublishing.com.

9. *College Prowler*, a series of paperbacks on individual colleges, written by students attending these institutions. Over 200 schools are rated on such topics as academics, local atmosphere, diversity, safety/security, computers, facilities, campus and off campus housing, parking, dating, etc. For example, *College Prowler—Case Western Reserve University, Cleveland, Ohio*, by Remy E. Olson, and Eds. Adam Burns, Matt Hamman, and Jon Skindzier, eds. Updated 9-12-07, College Prowler, Pittsburgh, PA, 800-290-2682, www.collegeprowler.com.

10. *Choosing the Right College, 2008–09: The Whole Truth About America's Top Schools*, by John Zmirak, editor-in-chief, an ISI Guide, Wilmington, DE, 2007.

11. *Colleges that Change Lives: 40 Schools that Will Change the Way You Think About Colleges*, by Loren Pope, Penguin Books, New York, N.Y. 2nd ed., 2006.

12. *Looking Beyond the Ivy League: Finding the Right College for You*, by Loren Pope, Penguin Books, New York, N.Y., revised, 2007.

13. *The Best Business Schools' Admission Secrets*, by Chigma Isiadinso, Sourcebooks, Inc., Naperville, IL, 2008, 630-961-3900, www.sourcebooks.com.

14. *Student's Guide to Colleges: the Definitive Guide to*

*America's Top 100 Schools; Written by the Real Experts—the Students Who Attend Them,* by Jordan Goldman and Colleen Buyers, Penguin Books, New York, N.Y. 2006, www.studentsguide.com.

15. *What High Schools Don't Tell You (and Parents Don't Want You to Know),* by Elizabeth Wissner-Gross, a Plume Book Educational Reference, Penguin Books, New York, N.Y. 2008, www.penguin.com or www.whathighschoolsdonttellyou.com.

16. *Countdown to College: 21 To-Do Lists for High School: Step by Step Strategies for 9, 10, 11 and 12th Graders,* by Valerie Pierce with Cheryl Rilly, Front Porch Press, Lansing, MI, 2nd ed., 2009; 517-487-9295, e-mail: styler@voyager.net.

17. *Get into College,* by Rachel Korn, and Jennifer Yetwin Kabat, sr., editors, Hundreds of Heads Books, Atlanta, GA, 2009, www.hundredsofheads.com.

18. *How to Survive Your Freshman Year: by Hundreds of College Students Who Did,* 3rd ed., by Frances Northcutt, special editor, created by Mark W. Bernstein and Yadin Kaufmann, Hundreds of Heads Books, Atlanta, GA, 2008, www.hundredsofheads.com.

19. *Community College Guide: the Essential Reference From Application to Graduation,* by Debra Gonsher, Dallas, TX, BenBella Books, 2009.

20. *Get Into Any College: Secrets of Harvard Students, Sixth Edition,* by Gen and Kelly Tanabe, Belmont, CA, Super College, LLC, 2006.

21. *Forbes* magazine's "America's Best Colleges," August 2009, see www.forbes.com.

22. *College Essays that Make a Difference,* 3rd ed., by the staff of *The Princeton Review,* New York, N.Y., Random House, 2008, www.princentonreview.com.

23. *Next Step College: Planning and Preparing for Ninth*

*and Tenth Graders* and *Next Step College: Applying and Deciding for Eleventh and Twelfth Graders*, Great Lakes Higher Education Guaranty Corporation. Visit www. mygreatlakes.org a nonprofit organization serving more than 2,700 schools, and 1,400 lenders across the nation. They are headquartered in Madison, Wisconsin.

24. *Association Directories*: check to see if your state publishes a directory of colleges. For example, the Association of Independent Colleges and Universities in Ohio (AICUO); see www.aicuo.edu.

Note that there are other ratings sources for specific disciplines. For instance, *Business Week*, www.businessweek.com.; *The Financial Times* (London), *The New York Times,* and the *Wall Street Journal*, all rate business schools both here and around the globe. The ratings are usually done on a yearly basis. All these publications are available at better bookstores and libraries. Occasionally, the national newspapers such as *The New York Times*, and *USA Today*, will publish parts of the data from the major evaluation sources. For example, the January 8, 2009 edition of *USA Today* published "Best Value Colleges: 50 Public and 60 Private Colleges and Universities," quoting *The Princeton Review*. Use the websites for these publications to check for the latest surveys. For example, search *Business Week*, www.businessweek.com.

Part B: Guides to Financing Your Education

1. *The Ultimate Scholarship Book, 2010: Billions of Dollars in Scholarships, Grants and Prizes*, by Gen and Kelly Tanabe, Super College, LLC, Belmont, CA, 2010. www.supercollege.com.

2. *1001 Ways to Pay for College: Practical Strategies to Make Any College Affordable*, by Gen and Kelly Ta-

nabe, Super College, LLC, Belmont, CA, 2009, www. supercollege.com.

3. *The College Solution: a Guide for Everyone Looking for the Right School at the Right Price*, by Lynn O'Shaughnessy, Prentice-Hall, Upper Saddle River, NJ, June 2008.

4. *Scholarships: Millions of Dollars in Free Money for College*, 2008 ed., by Gail Schlachter, R. David Weber, and the staff of Reference Service Press, Kaplan Publishing, New York, N.Y. 2008, www.kaplanpublishing. com; also, see www.rspfunding.com.

5. *The Princeton Review Paying for College Without Going Broke*, 2009 ed., Random House, New York, N.Y. 2009, 800-273-8439, www.princetonreview.com/bookstore.

6. Sallie Mae, *How to Pay For College: A Practical Guide for Families*, by Gen and Kelly Tanabe, Super College, LLC, Belmont, CA, 2008, www.supercollege.com.

7. *College Solutions ... a Roadmap to Selecting Your Best Strategy to Fund College and Retirement Without Going Broke*, by Rick Darvis, Phoenix, AZ, Stone People Publishing, 2005, see www.niccp.com.

8. For student loans: assistance information is available from the National Consumer Law Center; see www.borrowerassistance.org.

9. *Paying for College: Investing in your Future* by Great Lakes Higher Education Guaranty corporation; visit www.mygreatlakes.org., a nonprofit organization.

10. Great Lakes Educational Loan Service, Inc., is a subsidiary of the Great Lakes Higher Education Corporation in Madison, WI, see www.mygreatlakes.org, or phone 1-800-247-0482.

11. *The Complete Idiot's Guide to Paying for College* by Ken Clark, Alpha Group of Penguin Bantam, New York, N.Y. 2010.

# 4

# Where Do You Live?

First, the obvious. If you are attending a local college, you might need or want to live at home for financial, and other reasons. This short chapter is written for those who are leaving home, as where you choose to live will be a major factor in having a successful college career.

Wisely, many schools still require you to live in a dorm for one or two years. This ensures at least some supervision and, if you select the food option, a better diet (not necessarily a better-tasting one). I have always advised students to live on campus in dorms, fraternities, sororities, or special-interest boardinghouses on campus (often called co-ops), so that the student is immersed in the total campus life experience. As Dr. Ronald Berkman, President of Cleveland State University, states, "Students who live on campus become more engaged in the life of the campus and ultimately become stronger alums."[23] Living on campus also makes attending classes and events far more convenient, and you can walk or bicycle, both cheap and healthy activities. I have never liked to have students live "off campus" in typical rundown boardinghouses, where they usually only get to know two or three roommates, and seldom participate in campus events, such as dances, extracurricular interest groups, drama-music productions, and various festivals.

---

23. Janet Okoben, "Commuter School No More: CSU to Start Work This Week on New Dorms," *Plain Dealer,* Cleveland, OH, p. 1., August 24, 2009, jokoben@plaind.com.

Boardinghouses are fine for married and graduate students, but there isn't anything unique about living in an apartment, so why do it? You could, and some of you will, spend the rest of your life in apartments. I also wonder about the lack of supervision and God only knows about the food; I suspect pizza and breakfast foods, three times a day, seven days a week, plus too much booze. You cannot be a constant drinker and maximize your potential. Obviously the same warning applies for drugs, lack of sleep, poor diet, and other unhealthy habits. Remember, you are not bullet-proof!

If you must live off campus, make sure you participate in major campus events, and at least one student club. Expanding your circle of friends and sampling various campus activities is a very important part of your educational and personal development.

## Dorms and Other University-Authorized/Sponsored Housing

I've already mentioned some merits of on-campus living but I now want to comment on the value of learning to live with a roommate. While university housing advisors attempt to make reasonable matches, making adjustments to different personalities and habits is a key step in developing good social skills. Just as you will have to learn to work with all kinds of people, it's also good training for marriage/living with a partner. You will indeed have a more interesting, enjoyable, and productive life if you learn to appreciate and understand a wide variety of people. The same value can be said for foreign travel, and/or travel of any kind. Diverse experience helps develop coping, empathy, and flexibility, all great skills for handling a wide variety of people and situations.

We all have family and/or friends who are only comfortable with people identical to them—they all dress, act, speak, look and

66

think alike; that is not only very comfortable, but very comforting, however, with hardly any mind expansion. Even more harmful, these "same-set people" seem to develop unhealthy prejudices and biases toward anybody "not like them." We learn more from "different" people than we do from our own kind, who usually agree with what we think about most topics—very comfortable but not expanding our experience.

## Fraternities and Sororities

They have been around since the 1840s, and some chapters are good, some are bad. One must check on a chapter's particular campus reputation and history. If you walk in during a fraternity's "rush," the membership-drive period, and see a bar in the living room, you should be very suspicious. If the members only talk about booze, parties, sex, and pranks, move on to another "house," as fraternities are often called. Is there any supervision such as a housefather or housemother? I think almost all sororities have a housemother, but the fraternities that need it the most, vary widely on having adult supervision living in the house. At Michigan in Ann Arbor, I was a proud member of Phi Gamma Delta (it's a lifelong membership), where members are also known as "Fiji's" and "Phi Gams," but for me, that was a long time ago, and chapters change over time and keep on changing or evolving. For fraternities, ask the sorority girls, as they know what kind of guys are in each house. For sororities, I think the girls are much more astute at deciding on their own, as to whether the girls in a particular house are their kind of girls, whether they fit or not. They know better than to ask the fraternity guys, who probably only know which girls are cute and/or hot. One more time, up to the age of almost thirty, in maturity, girls are ahead of most boys, by about five years. Notice, I said "most" as there are always many exceptions.

In particular, check on each fraternity's concept of what used

67

to be called "hell week," or the physical test period, prior to final acceptance and initiation. Some chapters of fraternities still conduct crude "hazing" treatments, including pressure-tests involving excessive and forced alcohol consumption, which over the past few years even resulted in deaths at one or two fraternities. While all national headquarters of fraternities have long ago outlawed hazing, in favor of community service, a few local chapters seem to be run by extremely immature "party animals" and juvenile alcoholics. Obviously, stay away from these dysfunctional chapters, which even include a few sororities. Yes, there are some "bad girls" who usually team up with "bad guys."

When considering fraternities, sororities, and other group housing on campus, look for common interests, life style, majors, and other factors that fit your personality. If you are pre-med and most of the actives (initiated members versus pledges) are majoring in "advanced relaxation," and the place reminds you of an animal house, find a better fit. The reputations of fraternities are much more widely discussed than sororities, so ask around. For the girls, watch for the "snob" factor in sororities; you will instantly feel and see it, depending on how they look, talk, and act. Is this sorority chapter sort of a "Barbie doll house," with most of the sisters looking for "Ken," or are they serious about their education, and do they focus on character, as opposed to how you look?

The advantages of these fraternal groups include an instant group of friends, a comfortable home atmosphere, and a support system. Most stress scholarship, good study habits, tradition, history, an active social life, comradeship, and networking for life. The principles of these fraternal orders are noble, as they were developed during the nineteenth century, the last days of chivalry, which some still follow, and some don't. Select the right one for you; it can be a plus to college life. The university also has fraternal advisors and an inter-fraternity council (IFC), and an inter-sorority council (Panhellenic). Ask officers of these inter-councils regarding reputation and history for the various houses on campus.

One more advantage of fraternal groups is it's fun to iden-tify with fellow members who became famous in many fields, and they are good role models. Finally, a few small private colleges seem dominated by fraternity-sorority members, but I think less so today than in the 1950s. One of our most popular students at the University of Michigan, in Ann Arbor, who was the captain of the 1954 Michigan football team, always said and, still does at reunions, "I'm proud to be a GDI, (God Damn Independent)." The larger the school, the less influence there is from fraternal orders. There are many other ways to "socialize," just make sure they are positive experiences and activities.

If you simply cannot afford university/fraternal housing, make sure you do not restrict your friends to only your boarding house or apartment roommates. You could still expand your inter-action with a wide variety of students via extracurricular activi-ties, and by attending a reasonable number of campus functions. Remember, for the most part, social skills are learned out of class.

Chapter 5 gives a short summary of the major individuals, with whom you will have interaction: the advisors, administrators, and faculty, who will control your progress, and indeed, some of these characters are "characters."

# 5

# The Cast of "Characters" You Will Meet

You are going to meet and interact with a whole host of interesting people. Here is a list of the typical college cast of "characters," in the great play we call, "Going to College." While this might not seem important, it helps if you have some idea to whom you are talking, a prudent practice to develop for use throughout life. Perhaps as important, you will interact with most of the following members of the academic community:

1. Admissions: these will probably be the first individuals you will meet, either at a college-fair, open house, or on the campus. They are friendly, helpful, and will answer your questions about what the college has to offer, and help you complete your application.
2. Business administration and the registrar: finance and registration staffs are the major, nonacademic people you will meet. They will help you "matriculate," but don't worry, it is not a disease, but rather how you officially enroll, and how to pay tuition and fees.
3. Academic and financial counselors/advisors: their titles pretty well speak for themselves. These people will explain majors, minors, prerequisites, financial aid, how to use the library/labs, student clubs/activities, and the like.
4. Housing dorm advisors: these are board and room advisors, regarding living and eating plans, contracts, rules/regulations, fees, roommate selection, and the like.

70

5. Medical—the university health center: hopefully, you won't need this service, but a campus is like a city and has a "dispensary clinic," where you can be treated for minor problems, usually as an outpatient. There is also psychiatric counseling, along with general medical advice.
6. Security: you will see them, as most, but not all, are in uniform. Obviously they are there to help and protect you. They deserve your respect.
7. Maintenance and landscaping: God loves these fine, hardworking people who keep the campus looking beautiful. When appropriate, say "Thanks."
8. Academic officers: the usual "rank" order is as follows:

President (some universities use the title "Chancellor," but usually for the president of several connected campuses): the campus's chief executive officer (CEO) is mainly a fund-raiser, a public relations person, a referee, and final decision-maker. In public institutions, they also engage in state/public relations, lobbying among government officials, to maintain and increase financial support. At the large research-oriented universities, they also lobby for research grants. Ordinarily, you will only meet the president at major campus events where he or she is a kind of an adult academic cheerleader.

Vice presidents: these are in the areas of finance, administration, development (fund-raising), etc. You will not interact with these officials, nor will they want you to.

The provost: he or she is the chief academic officer of the college, to whom all the deans report. This is a very tough, demanding job and the only people who do it are those aspiring to be college presidents. At any one point in time, at least one campus group is fighting with the provost.

Deans: they are are the CEOs of the university's sub-colleges, and/or schools such as Arts and Sciences, Law, Medicine, Business, Education, Engineering, Music, Agriculture, etc. You will see a lot of these hard-working individuals who provide focus, vision, and hard-core leadership for their respective faculty, staff members, and students.

Department heads are called "chairs": these supervisors are combination administrators and faculty. They usually teach at least one course per semester, and "attempt" to manage the faculty. You will have lots of interaction with these dedicated individuals, who try to do a very tough job that most of their colleagues don't want.

Faculty: okay, now we are talking about the real power people in your college life. Here is the usual "rank" order:

Emeritus Professor: this person is a retired faculty member, voted by the department to this permanent title, and it means "retired from active service with honor." The president of the college is the final "approver" of this lifetime rank. You will obviously not interact with the "old farts."

Professors: these are the senior faculty members, and if you are at a smaller college—in particular, the small liberal arts colleges—you will have at least a few as instructors. They are tenured, which means they have successfully completed a five-to-seven year probationary period, have met the minimum requirements for their terminal degrees (most often, the Ph.D.), and have made many years of contributions to research, teaching, and service. If you are at a large research-oriented university, you will usually only interact with them in a large lecture session, with smaller "recitation" or labs taught by lesser ranks and/or

Ph.D. candidates, or teaching assistants (TAs). Some of you might occasionally have a "visiting professor," who will usually be a distinguished scholar from another institution, and who is temporarily teaching as a guest lecturer at the school you are attending.

Associate professor: this is a rank usually given at the same time the individual receives tenure. Tenure means the burden of proof for dismissal now rests with the institution. Unfortunately, it has come to mean, for most faculty, guaranteed life employment, and a few abuse this status. At one time and, I suspect it still is in effect in some regulations, tenure could be revoked because of moral misconduct, a financial crisis, and or physical impairment (inability to teach). This rank also almost always means the completion of the Ph.D, or some other terminal degree.

Assistant Professors: these are individuals recently hired from Ph.D.-granting institutions, who are starting on the tenure track for senior faculty positions. Many assistant professors have done what we call "all but the dissertation" (ABD), and are on a five-to-seven-year probationary program. Most are high-energy people, good teachers, and since they are usually in their late twenties, or early thirties, have a good rapport with students from their own generation.

Instructors and teaching assistants (TAs): some institutions use the rank of instructor for non-tenure-track teachers. If you are at a Ph.D.-granting institution (in your field), you will have teaching assistants who are graduate students with master's degrees, currently enrolled in their Ph.D. programs. Because they are very new at teaching, the quality of instruction varies quite a bit. As I indicated earlier, if English is their second language, you might have real trouble understanding them.

If many of your classmates are having the same problem, report it to the chair and, if necessary, further up the ladder. You have every right to expect understandable instructors.

Adjuncts—part-timers: with increasing costs and financial hard times, most institutions have increased the number of part-timers that some colleges call "adjuncts." They are usually people working full-time (some are retired), with at least a B.A. degree in their respective disciplines, and most are very good instructors—they like to teach, and share their extensive experience, and knowledge. Indeed, they usually have much more actual experience "doing" what they teach than full-time faculty, with business being the great example. The danger is, they can slip into mere descriptions of how their company or clinic operates, as opposed to a sampling of best practices and theory.

The department secretary: she—they are almost all female, unless brand new to the job—knows everything. I owe any administrative success I had, as a department chair, to several fine department secretaries. They always reminded me of the noncommissioned officer in charge (NCOIC), in the military. Those master sergeants and chief petty officers, who actually run their military units. Part of their value comes from the fact that even when the chair changes (usually after four to five five years), they remain. This means they know where all the bodies are buried, they have memorized all the rules and regulations, they know what works, but is not written down, and they are masters at understanding campus politics (they have to be in order to survive). They also supervise student assistants, and you might want to become one, for the experience and extra money. Treat the department secretary with great respect, and listen to what she tells you. Never, never get smart with these ladies, for they have more power than you realize. I want to pay a special tribute to my past department secretaries at California State University, Fresno. Doris Payne and Linda Vail, and to my entire staff at Capital University in Columbus, Ohio: Dottie Morrisroe, Carolyn Wang, Bonnie Coleman, Emma Lee, Laura Brown, and Trudy Rieser.

Let me now say a few words about the full-time faculty, the people who control your college destiny. First of all, if you think you had a few eccentric/strange teachers in high school, you haven't seen anything, yet! Because of the legitimate need to preserve academic freedom, colleges and universities have developed an exceptionally liberal capacity to accept and tolerate rather unconventional behavior, sometimes too tolerant. Compounding this freedom is the fact that faculty receive only minimal supervision. Tenure reinforces this attitude of liberal freedom, and some faculty takes advantage of it. This behavior could include the way they look, act, and other actions and habits, such as issuing shocking statements, displaying extreme political beliefs, and other eccentric behavior. However, in this day and age of permissive behavior, you might not be shocked, and you might even find some of this rather strange behavior interesting, as well as memorable.

Faculty people are known for their high egos, like many other gifted professionals, and some become "legends in their own minds." So what's the point? Feed their egos and avoid being a smart-ass, as you will never win this fight. Of course, there is a limit to this "freedom," such as inappropriate lecture material for the subject matter, frequently being unprepared, excessive absences from class, constant references to irrelevant personal and political views and obviously, sexual, racial, religious, and political harassment of any kind. Use your student evaluations and

75

other complaint procedures if "Dr. X" is really getting out of hand. But offer constructive criticism; do not use vitriolic language.

The good news is, you will meet at least two or three professors who will not only inspire you, but they will become true mentors and valuable counselors, usually for life. I still talk (at least once a year) to my Ph.D. mentors, Dr. I.V. Fine and Dr. Harland E. Samson, Professors Emeriti at the University of Wisconsin-Madison, and I miss several others, who have passed away, but I still remember their words of wisdom and the help they gave.

Well, as my British friends would say, "There you are." We are now ready for the next chapter, "How to Survive College," and remember, no one ever told you it would be easy (I hope!).

# 6

# How to Survive College

"Never have so many paid so much, and demanded so little."
                                    —author unknown (at least to me).

The quote cited above is well known and uttered by many faculty people. It means that many students spend a lot of money, either their own or somebody else's, and then try very hard to avoid using the varied services they purchase. It has always amazed me that some students seldom came to class, which is the very essence of being a student.

Perhaps the initial advice is, don't have an unplanned marriage and/or child, whichever comes first. In this day and age, with all of our sex education, and anything-goes society, you should be able to have sex and fun without marriage and kids. There is plenty of time for that later in life, when you are prepared for such responsibilities. Besides, we are all married a very long time, and it's getting longer, as we live longer. Well, there I said it. I got married at age thirty-two, which allowed me to have lots of adventures, date lots of females, serve in the USAF, travel, explore lots of options, and complete my first two degrees. Remember, the first degree is the most difficult one, with a rather high risk of failure to complete (except for the Ph.D., but that's another book). Of course, if you are a reentering, older parent, the knot has been tied, one way or another, but you should now be mature enough to handle serious study. It should be obvious that the freshman year is the toughest year, for most college students.[24]

By all means, attend the freshman and/or new-student orientation session, and any transition from high school to college courses that might be offered. Here are some tips on how to survive college:

1. Remember you "take" professors, not courses. In the classroom, the instructor is God, so what she or he says is the word. Bitch/argue about something with the teacher in college, or get "snotty," and you are probably history, or at the least, the instructor will not volunteer to act as a good reference. This isn't high school, where you could run home to cry on your parents' shoulders, or complain to the assistant "touchy-feely" principal. There is no reason why you must "like" the professor, and vice versa. Oh, it helps if that is the case, but you are there to learn, not to cultivate a friendship. Never say to the instructor, "I do not have time to do the assignment," and if that's true, you should not be in the class and perhaps, you should not be in college. Time management is *your* problem/task, it is not the problem of the faculty. Call your instructor, "Mr., Dr., Professor," or what they tell you. *Never,* use first names. These are not your buddies, and while they might not say anything, why gamble?
2. You are not a customer. Regardless of what you might have heard or even read, you are not a customer at the institution. If you graduate, you will be a certified product of it. Put another way, you are not buying a degree, you are earning it. This difference is attitude and/or perception, which is an enormous difference, and affects your

---

24. *How to Survive your Freshman Year*, cited in chapter 3, in the appendix.

willingness to compete for the "rights and privileges," of a graduate.

3. Studying is hard work. Mastering most subject matter of any significance requires hours of concentrated effort in reading, calculating, preparation, thinking, lab work, and writing. No one ever told you that school, at any level, would be easy, fun and games, fast, or simple. If you "got by" in high school by being cute, popular, good in athletics, or by taking easy courses, and being in a noncompetitive environment, you are now in for a shock. Some of you, in this category, will wake up to the challenge, others will go home. Don't be a quitter. Get down to work. Don't waste either your or someone else's money.

4. Carefully read your course outlines (syllabus) and schedule for assignments and exams, including starting and finishing dates for studying, papers, and projects. Enter these dates in your Blackberry, desk calendar, laptop, or whatever you use as a planning and scheduling tool. Schedule and write down daily tasks that you must do that day, and future key due dates, for the entire semester. Remember to priortize your tasks in order of importance, difficulty, and time required to complete. Like high school (I hope), you must complete your assignments/homework on time. Use the time between classes for studying, doing research, and to write.

5. Read the assignment before class, or at least skim the material, so you can take better notes, and ask proper questions.

6. Go to class. Wow, is this far out! Absences beyond four will get you into real trouble, especially back-to-back misses. To your own embarrassment, and to the disgust of other students, soon you will start to ask questions on materials already covered. You or somebody paid to

have you go to class, so for heaven's sake, do it, whether the instructor cares or not. In particular, to get a good start, make sure you attend the first class as it includes the course orientation. If you have changed courses within the allowed time period, the burden is on you to obtain past lecture notes. You'd better have a friend in the added course, as professors are under no obligation to give you lecture notes, only material handed out in class.

7. Try to review your lecture notes each day. I know this is tough, but review what you wrote while it is still fresh in your memory. Correct and fill in the missing information, and make notes of what to ask the professor. In particular, record those clues as to what is important, and what might be on the exam.

8. We learn more from our mistakes than our successes. That's because they have more emotional impact. While you might be shocked at all those red marks on your first term paper, if you were perfect, you would not need the class. If your skin is too thin to take accurate criticism, this means you are not coachable and probably should not be in college. As I said previously, you must have humility to learn. This is college and it should be much more rigorous and competitive than the typical high school, and the lazy students are gone.

9. Learn to be a good listener. Good listening is one of the key facilitators of effective learning, and it means we understand, versus just hearing. You could actually take classes on "How to be a better listener" and, aside from making you a better conversationalist, you will learn more. Good listening requires an objective mind-set and concentration. Taking notes helps to focus attention on what you are hearing, and reinforces understanding, and its meaning. We all know some individuals who allow

too much emotion to interfere with listening, critical thinking, and rational/logical problem solving.

10. The learning function of repetition and outlining. You learned in high school how to memorize facts, formulas, speeches, play skits, football plays, foreign languages, songs, etc., you also learned that to memorize, you must go over the material several times, sometimes many times, whether you repeat it verbally, reread it, or rewrite it. Go beyond the memorizing, and develop the ability to find the real meaning behind the words.

I think it helps to write an outline of the major points in your textbook and handout, as the mere act of writing the outline helps you to memorize it, provokes thinking, and it provides an excellent review source for examinations. If you are taking a speech class, find a private place and give your speech over and over to the walls, or perhaps a friend. Cue sheets such as four-by-six cards could help you master the material, just as flash cards help in the study of foreign languages, formulas, definitions, and other such data.

11. Learn the language of the subject matter. Every field of study, profession, and vocation has its own unique set of terms, definitions, and word meanings specific to the particular discipline. For instance, if you are studying quality control in a business operations course or in engineering, the term "black belt" means an achievement level within the Six-Sigma QC training programs. It has nothing to do with jujitsu or wrestling. You must learn to use such terms with precision and in proper places in your essay answers, papers, and objective answers on various tests. During the reviews of test results, it will not matter if you say, "Well, I meant to write..." You either can use the correct words and terms in the proper context, or you can't. This is just another reason why

you must memorize certain words, concepts, definitions, and terms in specific courses.

12. Thinking and reasoning beyond memorization. While you were introduced to the practice of rational thought, logic, and problem solving in a high school, you must now develop these skills and abilities with much more sophistication and depth. As preparation, try to take at least one logic or problem-solving technique course, such as argumentation, debate, or negotiation. Most business, engineering, and other technical courses teach at least some problem-solving skills, including differentiation between facts and assumptions, criteria determination, analysis, testing of alternatives, selection of solutions, and execution/action steps. These courses, plus experience, help develop good judgment, wisdom, and confidence.

13. Never get behind more than one week in any one subject. Work first, then play but all students have some schedule disruptions due to extracurricular activities, field trips, or spiking workloads in other courses. I always used either Saturday morning to catch up with the missed reading, or some other open time in my schedule. In fact, I used Thanksgiving and Christmas vacations to write/finish papers. Again, use that time between classes to read, write, and to do research.

14. Find a quiet place to read/study. I used the main Michigan Law Library—somewhat illegal for undergrads—because it was dead quiet, and silence was enforced by the serious and more mature law students. Besides, it is one of the most beautiful Tudor Gothic English halls on the campus, and inspires intellectual endeavor. I do not believe one can seriously study with the radio or TV on, let alone be distracted by side conversations with other

students. If you have your own room, wonderful. I never did until graduate school.
15. See your professor for help early on. Don't wait until one week before finals if you are having trouble. Their job is to help you, but they can't help you, if you don't see them, with sufficient lead time. See them during their office hours or by appointment. This must be done in time to help you understand the material, assignments, and other issues, such as handling exams. I know it is embarrassing to admit when we are in trouble and need help, but the smart people do it.
16. Pick your friends carefully. I could have started with this point, as you must socialize with serious students. If you hang out with drinkers and other party animals, you will probably be home by the end of the six-week exams, or at the latest, at the end of the semester,. Many of these party professionals never wanted to go to college in the first place, and are simply waiting to quit or flunk out. Select positive, fun people, but find the responsible ones with good judgment, those who share your goals and value system. Also, as in all aspects of life, we are often judged by the company we keep. I think we pick up their habits, including how they speak, dress, and act. Make sure your friends have good habits.
17. Preparing for and taking exams. High school prepared you for the basics of study and, as I always reminded my students, if everything else fails, read the textbook. College exams are much more intense and cover more material. Start your preparation early enough to finish the task, but all college students have to "burn the midnight oil" once in a while. Beware of a few fellow students who boast that they never study, as many are "sandbaggers." These are students who study a lot but hope to trick you into not studying, in order to improve

their chances of getting higher scores. Understand how competitive college can be.

Almost all professors give clues as to what will be on the exams. Pay attention to anything he or she says, such as, "This is a major point," or, "This is a key concept for you to learn," etc. Usually, anything said, presented in a PowerPoint, written on the board, in the textbook, or given to you in a handout, could be on the exams. The good news is that many professors hold review sessions prior to major exams such as midterms and finals.

Unless there are penalties for wrong answers on those multiple choice and true/false tests, by all means guess. Watch your time, do not spend too much time on any one question; go on, and then go back to it, if you have time. You must remember that most objective tests call for the best answer, not the only answer. Usually the correct answer is the course/teacher answer or "school solution," as we so often hear. One good tactic is to first eliminate the options that you know are wrong. Whether you agree with the correct response or disagree is immaterial; don't argue with the exam.

Acute nerves over taking tests? The better prepared you are, the less nervous you will be. Some colleges offer students the opportunity to test alone to reduce anxiety, so check the regulations as to the procedure.

Essay exams usually require the answer to be in a structured outline. For example, you might write that there are four major factors to consider: 1 _____, 2 _____, 3 _____, and 4 _____. Try not to ramble, as the professor has just so much time to read your answer, and will quickly give up if he or she starts to suspect pure 'BS.' The scoring is usually on a point basis and, by definition, is very subjective. If you want to argue in class when the "blue books" (exam pamphlets) are handed back, be polite and see the professor in his or her office for further explanations.

Remember, teachers grade on results, not effort. It does not matter how hard you worked or that you "did all the assignments." As in all aspects in life, you will always be evaluated on how well you do a particular task, and someone will always be the "evaluator." This is much like the reality that effort counts in athletics, only *if you win*. Remember, our Declaration of Independence states that we only have the right to *pursue* happiness, not simply to have it. We have the right to compete, not to win. Also, the referee is the teacher. I recall being in one class as an undergrad and a rather brash student said, "I do not see how the correct answer is relevant." The professor merely said, "Young man, our task at this university is to make *you* relevant." Teachers are trained, paid, and expected to render a verdict on how well you are performing. Much of this grading is inherently subjective and, obviously, the judgment of the instructor is better than yours. No one "deserves" a good grade, it must be earned and a positive attitude is a big factor in academic success.

Remember, "C" means "Average," and most of us are average in at least some skill areas. To think you are "A," that is "excellent," or even "B," that is "very good," in all subjects, is probably false and this arrogant attitude will inhibit learning. Even those individuals we describe as "brilliant" could be "D," that is "unsatisfactory," or even "F," that is "failures," in at least some subjects.

Most instructors will not negotiate about grading. While it is now popular to appeal grades, they should not be changed, except for what is known as a mechanical error on straight objective tests. This means the total point count might be wrong, the grading key could have slipped, or an answer was overlooked. Grading of essays and short answers is inherently subjective, and it is not always what you write, but how you write it. As I mentioned before, we are all constantly judged by someone, throughout our lives, so get used to it. If you argue with your boss when you are working, you will probably be terminated or at least "passed over," because of a bad attitude. On the other hand, do see your instructor if you do not understand your grade or score. Find out what you need to do in order to improve.

The good news is, one or two of your professors will inspire, challenge, and coach you to be "all you can be" in a particular subject. I still recall, forty to sixty years later, the advice and guidance of several former professors, and none of them were easy graders. In fact, they were like all great coaches, they were demanding.

Watch the scribbling and incorrect spelling, although most faculty will permit abbreviations, and some poetic license. Your instructor should give you adequate guidelines regarding test taking in the particular course. For example, in English courses, you might indeed be asked to write a real essay or "story," without an outline.

For true/false questions, my best advice is to think what is mostly true or mostly false, as many of these questions could be a case of, "It depends." The more you know about a subject, the more trouble you will have with true/false questions.

*Finally, no cheating or plagiarism. This unethical behavior will come back to haunt you. It's always on your record and could result in your instant dismissal from the institution!!!!* While it might be trite, you are only cheating yourself. Good grades must be earned with intellect and hard work.

18. Writing papers. First of all, write them yourself. Under no circumstances should you pay and/or have anybody do your work. For one thing, it constitutes plagiarism, which we just discussed. Plagiarism is grounds for immediate dismissal from most colleges, or at least from the course. Furthermore, you are cheating yourself. Learning to write well is a key skill needed in most vocations. It ranks up there with the ability to speak well, and both constitute the ability to effectively communicate.

All writers suffer from the "blank page syndrome," at least once in a while. This paralysis of "not starting" can be solved using the following techniques:

a. Jot down a few ideas, possible themes, annotated notes, sources, thoughts, questions, anything to get you started. Imagine, dream, think, and do not worry about the writing style, spelling, or punctuation.

b. Start writing, and organize, structure, and document later. You must start to break the writer's block, as it is often called. Use the language of the course.

c. Now go back and structure with headings and subheadings, if you are writing a typical subject-research paper. If it's a classic essay, correct for transition, flow, style, and meaning.

d. Correct the grammar and punctuation. See any number of editorial-style guides such as *The Chicago Manual of Style* (University of Chicago Press), and/or the classic reference *A Manual for Writers of Term Papers, Theses, and Dissertations*, by Kate L. Turabian (University of Chicago Press), or one recommended by your professor, or the college. Even a suitable college-level dictionary will have an appendix on editorial style.

e. Check for original sources. The Internet transmission time and date may not give the source of the data. Who is the author? What is the real title of the work, the place and name of the publisher, the publication date, the pages?

f. Write at least two drafts.

g. Have a good writer friend review your work.

At the risk of being redundant, I think the success factors leading to good writing include outlining the major and sub-points. Now start writing several drafts to ensure proper thought expression, flow, transition, correct grammar, punctuation, and spelling. When you get your papers back with corrections noted in red, don't get defensive. Good writing usually requires many drafts. Yes, it is hard work, but rewarding. Take the advice and learn how to write better. Finally, remember "spell check" and most other computer programs can't conjugate verbs, or resolve several other grammar issues, such as using incorrect words or proper punctuation, within the context of the paper. Finally, remember that references mean documentation from original sources, not from Internet data sites, unless they are all quoting original sources with full documentation. This is becoming a major problem and the Internet has become a huge source of incorrect and fabricated information.

19. Do you need a tutor?—most colleges have student tutors available for small fees, and they could be especially useful in math, science, foreign-language study, and to help you develop better study skills. Check with the proper office at your college.

20. Taking tough courses (tough for you). There is a normal tendency to keep taking courses you are good at, versus

courses you need. I'm not talking about necessary pre-requisites or required courses in your major. I'm talking about avoiding the math or English composition course you really need, but don't have to take. For example, if you can't handle ordinary math problems, take the courses to conquer this deficiency as this weakness will hurt you all your life. Okay, take these courses as pass/fail, but do take them. If you are paralyzed while speaking in front of a group, take a course in public speaking.

21. Exploring subjects. The first two years of most traditional college programs, require what we used to call the general education (GE) requirements. These include courses in the basic foundation courses in math, history, science, English, social science, and a few other essentials, to prepare you for advanced study. The objective is to make you a balanced person, and to help you determine what is of interest to you, for a possible major and minor. Think of this as an opportunity to sample the menu of life.

22. The role/value of extracurricular activities. Many advisors rightfully state that out-of-class campus activities represent the other half of the college education. There are numerous subject-interest clubs, like the Spanish club or the student marketing club, for you to meet other students with similar interests, and engage in interesting and educational activities. There are many "service" fraternities, honorary societies, student government councils, and other student organizations that will enrich your college experience. Employment recruiters look for evidence that you did more than you had to do. This is a logical extension of my previous advice, to participate in all aspects of college life. One more caution about heavy-time-commitment activities, such as sports, music, and drama. You will need to be very disciplined

and an excellent time manager, but most feel it's worth it. I know I did, as a member of the Michigan Union Board of Directors at the University of Michigan, in Ann Arbor, where I learned key management and leadership skills. By the way, you can still work your way through college, and participate in at least a few extracurricular activities. At the minimum, you should belong to the student club in your discipline.

Finally, as I have suggested before, it's okay to change your major even if it adds a semester or two to your college career. Better to pursue what you want to do and like, rather than entering a vocation you no longer desire. For one thing, you will not excel at what you do not like. Many people have several different careers over their lifetime. A few of you might even find it productive to take a semester off and work, travel, or simply research what you want to do with the rest of your life. I have suggested to more than one student, "Take some time off, and contemplate your navel." The overseas study programs are a wonderful experience and a semester abroad is often a great way to open up your mind to new paths to follow.

Our final chapter, quite appropriately, is about commencement and the typical questions about work or graduate school and life after college. These topics are indeed introduced at the end of this book, and notice, I have used a word "introduced," since the major theme of this book is about starting college, not starting work or graduate school—that's for another book. However, I just have to give at least some advice on the subject of "Life after the bachelor's degree."

# 7

# Commencement and What's the Next Step, Work or Graduate School?

First, aside from your special studies in your major and minor, what have you learned? Whether you can articulate it or not, you have, or should have, learned how to think with rational logic, how to solve problems, how to be objective, how to separate the emotional and irrational from the truth/facts and, hopefully, to have much better judgment. Second, you should speak and write much better than you did on your first day at college. Third, you should have much more appreciation for the fine arts, music, philosophy, economics, history, science, and theater. Fourth, you should be a more interesting person with good social skills and etiquette. Fifth, you most certainly should be a better communicator. Finally, all of us in academia hope you will be better citizen, and that you will contribute something back to society, and leave a positive footprint. By the way, if I were you, I would keep key reference textbooks for on-the-job training and, as a review source for graduate school, prerequisites and core courses. Learn to start your own personal and professional library.

Your degree is, as we have noted before, a door opener for lots of opportunities. These include job opportunities, and volunteer positions to serve your fellow man. Commencement means "the beginning," even though we associate it with the end of a school program. Do attend your commencement, not just because your parents want it, but because you have earned the right to be there, to share in the excitement of a memory that will last a lifetime. It is like many of life's other events and opportunities—they come but once, so do not miss your commencement. If you do, you will regret it years later.

What's the next step, work or graduate school? For many of you in pre-graduate programs such as pre-law, pre-medicine, pre-Ph.D., and other such "prep" programs, you are obviously off to graduate school to finish your professional-degree requirements. If you are a business major, I, like many graduate business schools, recommend you work for at least two years before pursuing your M.B.A., or even the Ph.D. in business. Another benefit of working while pursuing an evening/weekend degree, is the possibility of receiving tuition reimbursement from your employer. Business is an operational occupation, and the practical work experience will help you to be a much better business analyst, or case writer, and you will know what questions to ask in the advanced courses. In short, the M.B.A. degree will have much more impact on you, and considerably more value will be added. The selection of where to go to graduate school is best left to the recommendation by one or two of your favorite professors. The guides listed in chapter 3, in the appendix, also contain ratings on graduate schools.

If you are planning on first working, when you interview, find out which organizations have tuition reimbursement for graduate school. For those of you going to work, I assume you have already contacted your school or department placement office for advice on résumé preparation, interviewing skills, and appointments with organizations, either coming to the campus, or posting job opportunities on their websites. While I'm sure your employment counselors will cover interviewing skills, here is my list of big mistakes to avoid during the personal interview, either for graduate school or employment:

1. Do your homework—study reports and material about the organization, well ahead of the interview. Make a copy of their website. Proper preparation will provide

the basis for astute questions. Make sure you know their mission statement, charter, history, the product/service line, geographical locations of their operations, and obvious data such as sales, number of employees, ownership, etc.

2. Be early.
3. Dress for the job. If in doubt,, wear a conservative dress, a pressed suit and a tie, or a sport coat and a tie. If male, take your hat off. Gentlemen do not wear hats inside. No gum, and have an appropriate haircut/hairdo. If possible, find out how the organization dresses, looks, and then emulate, to the extent possible. Their website might reveal what the employees and managers "look like."
4. Watch your posture. Sit up straight.
5. Call the interviewer "Mr., Ms., Mrs., Dr.," or by the person's title, unless the person corrects you. I know we live in a very casual country, but avoid being over-familiar like the obnoxious telemarketers. In particular, some businesses are more formal than people suspect. Do not gamble. Start out with formal respect. Ask for their business card. If the interviewer says, "Call me Jane," then you can be informal and speak with more comfort.
6. Watch your English, grammar, slang, and tone. If you say, "It don't," "It ain't," "I seen," you are through. Educated people do not massacre the English language, and seldom use street slang. In addition, *how* you say things is as important as *what* you say, so watch your tone and voice inflection. I like the book *Managing Your Mouth*, by Robert L. Genua.[25]
7. Check your body language. One way to do this is to conduct a trial or "mock" interview with a friend or, better

25. Robert L. Genua, *Managing Your Mouth: an Owner's Manual for Your Most Important Business Asset*, New York, N.Y., AMACON, the American Management Association, 1992.

yet, a counselor or a faculty member. Your expressions will speak louder than your mouth. Smile, be positive, and look alert. Positive and appropriate facial expressions are key factors in successful interviews, negotiations, and day-to-day conversations.[26]

8. Ask pertinent questions. Using the data you researched on the Internet, or found in the career placement office, ask thoughtful questions regarding job duties, travel, tuition reimbursement for graduate school, in-house training, promotion opportunities and, yes, compensation and benefits (do this last). Ask about the products and services offered by the organization, including its history. Ask the interviewers about their careers in the organization—why did they join it, what do they like about the company—and other such questions that demonstrate your interest and preparation. Try to determine their culture, value standards, their personality—to see if you fit in.

9. Take notes—this shows attention and interest. You will also need them for later interviews, thank you notes, and after employment.

10. Don't talk too much. This is a tough judgment issue, but talk long enough to cover the subject, and short enough to be interesting. The mock session will provide good feedback on this point. In particular, do not brag or say negative comments about your school, faculty, friends, etc. Negative personal comments are in very bad taste, and provoke real questions regarding your attitude. Sell yourself in a pleasant way, by suggesting what particular skills you would bring to the job. I like the slogan

26. Read *The Tipping Point: How Little Things Can Make a Big Difference*, by Malcolm Gladwell, for a fascinating description of various persuasion factors, including body English, New York, N.Y., Back Bay Books/Little, Brown and Company, 2000, 2002, p.p. 89–132.

of the Emmy Award–winning TV news anchor, Connie Dieken, "Talk less, say more."[27]

11. If invited to lunch or dinner, watch your manners and etiquette—no elbows on the table, use the correct utensils, and no alcohol. If you are weak or nervous in this area, see *The Essential Manners for Men*, by Peter Post, New York, Harper/Collins, 2003, or Letitia Baldrige's *Complete Guide to the New Manners for the 90's*, New York, Rawson Associates, Macmillan Publishing Co., 1990, as men are usually the most vulnerable on this subject. As I mentioned in chapter 2, polish those social skills we call manners. Remember my earlier comments in chapter 2, about having "class" or "polish."

12. Thank the interviewer for the meeting, and ask about the next step—do you call, write, e-mail, or do they, and when or how?

13. Send a thank you note, preferably via a formal note, but at least by e-mail. One last job-placement comment, select your first job for how much you will learn versus how much you will earn. Learn to send thank you notes for any gift or special act of kindness you receive.

14. Learn from each interview. Do a postmortem. What went well? What did not? How could this interview have gone better, and what do you need to do for the next one? How can you be a better candidate?

27. Michael Heaton, "10 Minutes with ... Connie Dieken, Turning Into Action," from her book *Talk Less, Say More: 3 Habits to Influence Others and Make Things Happen*, Wiley, New York, N.Y. 2009, *The Plain Dealer*, Cleveland, OH, November 2, 2009, p. D3, mheaton@plaind.com.

# Concluding Thoughts

First, do not let your college education stand in your way of becoming a success. This is another way of saying that some attend and even graduate, without becoming "educated." Being educated does not just mean you have a degree. *Webster's New World College Dictionary*: Revised and Updated, 3rd Edition, 1996, defines "educated" as "having or showing the results of much education." Thus, the college degree gives most of those who have it the tools, knowledge, skills, and motivation to achieve results at doing "something." The college degree is basically a "door opener" but what really counts is how you walk through the many doors, and perform on this wonderful but challenging road of life. It is a great prep course for life, but it only works if we really learn, versus only mechanically going to class, with little or no participation in the total college life experience. Do not let this happen to you. Develop a passion to excel in all those courses, events, and experiences. By "passion," I mean the desire and ability to contribute, produce, and excel. Yes, you should be happy to finally earn your college degree, and while you should not want to remain on campus at the end of your degree work, I do want you to have most eyes at commencement.

Second, it's okay to fail. Most successful people have failed, at one time or another .What is important is how you respond to setbacks. As I've suggested before, learn from your mistakes. Pick yourself up, do not blame others, correct the problem, and start over. Even if you leave college prior to earning a degree, on your first attempt, go back when you are ready. We are educated when we know what we do not know. The really dangerous people in the world are those who think they know it all and/or they have finished learning.

Third, and again, it's okay to change your vocational decision, there is plenty of time to alter your career. In addition, it's okay to take some time off after graduation, to have some fun—

you deserve it. I like the title of one guide book, *How to Survive the Real World*. And to a large degree, the typical college student in residence at a typical college is indeed living in a very special protective environment, preparing to enter real life.[28]

Regarding a proper ending for this book, it suddenly occurred to me that I had delivered on May 9, 2009, a closing, commencement-type dinner address to the XI Deuteron Chapter of Phi Gamma Delta, at Case Western Reserve University in Cleveland, Ohio. This dinner is called the "Pig Dinner."[29] The following is what I would share with you if you were in attendance, as I feel the remarks are appropriate for all college graduates, male or female. In fact, I used most of these points as the commencement speaker, at National College, June 6, 1987, at their Fresno, California, campus:

> In many respects, the Pig Dinner is the commencement exercise for the fraternity, as it is usually the last formal event for the active brothers. Thus I'm going to address my remarks primarily to senior Fiji's, who are leaving, in order to try to share with all of you my thoughts of what I think Phi Gamma Delta means to us, the charge our founding fathers gave us, the meaning of "Not for college days alone," way back in 1848.
>
> However, this evening is also an opportunity for the alumni brothers (old farts) to share with the actives, their memories, war

---

28. *How to Survive the Real World: Life After College Graduation*, by Andrea Syrtash, special editor, Hundreds of Heads Books, Atlanta, GA, 2006, www. hundredsofheads.com.

29. The Norris Pig Dinner is the annual alumni/active members dinner, celebrated by all the chapters of Phi Gamma Delta, since 1893, when it was first held by Frank B. Norris, at the University of California, in Berkeley. While Norris died an untimely death in 1902, he had already become a noted author. (Publisher's note: Professor Pinkerton was selected by his fellow students to be the student commencement speaker, at the University of Michigan's commencement in 1955, just as he was four years earlier at a high school in Cleveland, where he is a member of the Parma Senior High School Hall of Fame.)

stories, "Do you remembers," and other bragging rights. It is a form of bonding, hands-across-the-generations. Indeed, I will tell you one of my fond memories, from my time as a USAF veteran, returning to Case Western Reserve in my hometown (Parma Senior High School) as a student in the M.B.A. program (1960–1962). I can only tell it—nothing in writing to protect the virtue of the young coed, the lovely major character of the story, whom I shall call "Mary Mather."

Now, I want to share eleven of what I believe are appropriate marching orders for any attendees at a Norris Pig Dinner but, in particular, for the graduating seniors.

1.  Select your first job/position more for what you will learn versus earn. This initial foundation will pay off handsomely in the following years.
2.  Focus on your responsibilities rather than you rights. I still feel the best presidential quote was by President John F. Kennedy, "Ask not what your country can do for you, but what *you* can do for your country." I still believe in the oath I took as a new military officer, more than fifty-five years ago: "Duty, honor, God, and country."
3.  In every endeavor, conduct yourself with high ethical actions, integrity, virtue, and all the other high moral standards embodied in the creed of Phi Gamma Delta. I'm sad to observe the obvious: that our modern society has fallen to new lows in terms of personal conduct. Greed, arrogance, and self-centered mind-sets are destroying this country. You have an opportunity to restore honor and honesty. Remember, our official values are "friendship, knowledge, service, morality, and excellence."
4.  In addition, pay attention to good manners and what we call proper social graces. We are supposed to be "gentlemen," so look, dress, act, and talk like one. For starters, remove your hat when inside, and you can dress casual, without looking like you're homeless. Yes, there is "Dress beyond jeans." You will look and feel better, I guarantee

it. Most private clubs still have at least some dress codes. I know mine do.

5.  Give a damn—make a difference by joining various civic organizations; support sound local causes; be active in politics and the church; get involved in the PTA; the Boy Scouts; join Kiwanis, Rotary, etc.; pick one or two, and do something good for your city, county, state, and country. We expect educated people such as you to now join the ranks, and give back something positive to the government and society that gave you so much. Be a giver and not just a taker. Select a charity and/or cause, and support it. The Cleveland Art Museum, the Cleveland Orchestra, Playhouse Square, and other such institutions in this city, exist today because numerous civic-minded people came to their rescue. For me, it is the Hannah Neil Home for Children in Columbus, Ohio, a safe haven for neglected, and abused children.

6.  Reach out and help your brothers and sisters. Many of you, perhaps most, will supervise somebody, which I believe is a privilege. Take time to listen, observe, and help another person when he or she cries out. Go out of your way to help fellow workers, friends, or somebody in need, and you will be rich beyond your wildest dreams.

7.  Be an entrepreneur. Try to create something new: a patent, a concept, a new computer, a new company, a great novel, a new technique, a new tool, something innovative, and better. The opportunities to do that are even better today than years ago—witness all the young people who founded the generation of computer and software companies.

8.  Be a good alumnus of Case Western Reserve and Phi Gamma Delta. You are now a member, a life member, of this great institution, and our brotherhood. Support both, and be an active alumni member. Private institutions, in particular, need our strong and constant support, if we do not, who will? As soon as you can, be a Perge Society Member (members donating money to the schol-

arship fund). You might even be called to help "save your chapter," like Brothers Jack McKinnie (Ohio Wesleyan), Bob Niebaum (Case WRU), George Qua and Tom Eames (Michigan), Paul Qua (DePauw), and many others. God bless them!

9.  Keep on learning. Hopefully, you've learned how to learn, think, and solve problems, and what you don't know. Only the ignorant think "Class is over," and it is essential to keep reading, to go back to take special courses to prevent obsolescence, to expand your horizons, and to master new skills. Even the professional athletic teams constantly practice before every game, and you are now in the biggest game of all. Remember, our "Declaration of Independence" states we have the right to *pursue* happiness, not just to have it, and you will have to keep learning how to pursue it. We have the right to compete, not the guaranteed right to win. No one has or should have the right to win; it must be earned, achieved, and won. As a side note, I think the really evil discrimination was not allowing blacks, women, and other selected ethnic groups to even compete, to try for law school, medical school, sports, etc. Conversely, this is the reason I never favored quotas, which is an obvious reverse discrimination, and grants entry without merit.

10. Live a personal life of moderation, based on educated common sense. If you are drifting into substance abuse, seek professional help. Perhaps as important, if you detect that another person is on a self-destructive path, advise him or her to take a corrective action. Remember, mature people who care offer sound advice. Have friends who care, and to have a friend, you must be a friend. My fraternity brothers have told me for years to watch my weight and exercise more; I should have listened—maybe I could have avoided my recent open-heart surgery.

11. Finally, leave a positive footprint behind when you go up to Fiji heaven. This last item is actually the summation

of the other ten. What would you want your obituary to state? The great majority of us want to be remembered as someone who made a social-civic contribution, one who served others, one who cared for his or her fellow human beings, and someone who made a difference. Simply being wealthy makes people physically comfortable, but not necessarily happy, or remembered for much of anything. Perhaps the message is not so much what your assets are, but how you made them, and what you did with those assets, beyond your own self-gratification.

Well, I can see by the clock that my time is just about up, and yours is about to begin. "You will commence." At my first commencement I was rather startled when at the end of the ceremony, in the great University of Michigan stadium, they first played taps for the conclusion of one phase of our lives, and then reveille for the beginning of another. It is truly an honor to be with you, and share this fine conclusion to another exciting, and rewarding year in Phi Gamma Delta, and so I bring you both greetings and a good-bye, with a prayer for a safe journey into a beautiful tomorrow. One final thought to share with you is this lovely benediction called "The Irish Blessing":

"May the wind be always at your back,
May the sun shine warm upon your face,
The rain fall soft upon your fields
And until we meet again, may God hold you
In the palm of His hand."

Good luck, Godspeed, and fraternally,
Richard L. Pinkerton

## A Short List of Suggested Readings for Student Counselors, Administrators, and Serious Parents

1. *Real Education: Four Simple Truths for Bringing America's Schools Back to Reality*, by Charles A. Murray, New York, N.Y. Crown Forum, 2008. www.crownpublishing.com. This is a riveting, fast read about what's wrong with the U.S. education system, and why "Leave no children behind," does not and will not be successful. Its bibliography is extensive and the very best on the subject. Murray is known as the author of "two of the mostly widely debated and influential social policy books, in the last three decades." Note: *Real Education* is available as an eBook. The four truths he cites are: ability varies, half of the children are below average, too many people are going to college, and America's future depends on how we educate the academically gifted.
2. *Losing Ground: American Social Policy 1950–1980*, by Charles A. Murray, New York, N.Y. Basic Books, 1984.
3. *The Bell Curve Intelligence and Class Structure in American Life*, by Charles A. Murray and Richard J. Hernstein, New York, N.Y. The Free Press, 1994. Murray is the W.H. Brady Scholar at the American Enterprise Institute in Washington, DC.
4. *The Lowering of Higher Education in America: Why Financial Aid Should Be Based On Student Performance*, by Jackson Toby, Santa Barbara, Calif., Praeger, an imprint of ABC-CLIO, LLC, 2010. It is an excellent commentary on behavior of American high school students, grade inflation, "goofing off at college," and financial aid policy. Also available as an eBook; visit www.abc-clio.com.
5. *50 Rules Kids Won't Learn In School: Real World An-*

*tidotes to Feel-Good Education*, by Charles J. Sykes, New York, N.Y., St. Martin's Press, 2007.

6. *Dumbing Down Our Kids: Why American Children Feel Good About Themselves But Can't Read, Write, or Add*, by Charles J. Sykes, New York, N.Y., St. Martin's Press, 1995.

7. *Going Broke by Degree: Why College Costs Too Much*, by Richard K. Vedder, Washington, DC, AEI Press, publisher for the American Enterprise Institute, 2004. Dr. Vedder is a distinguished Professor of Economics at Ohio University in Athens, Ohio. A much-published author, he confirms what many faculty members have long suspected—many colleges and universities are very inefficient, with excessive overhead and, currently, overpaid administrators. In addition, some faculty members at the large research-oriented institutions simply do not teach enough courses. This same thesis is reinforced in an article, "Bureaucratic U Pay the Teachers, Not the Administrators," by Daniel L. Bennett, Administrative Director at The Center of College Affordability, and Productivity in Washington, DC, *Forbes*, July 13, 2009, p. 24.

8. *Higher Education in Transition: A History of American Colleges and Universities, 1636–1956*, by John S. Brubacher and Willis Rudy, New York, N.Y. Harper and Brothers Publishers, 1958. Brubacher was a Professor of History and Philosophy of Higher Education, at Yale and Rudy was a Professor of History, at the State Teachers College, in Worcester. This is a very interesting work, starting with the development of the colonial colleges (Harvard, Yale, William and Mary, New Jersey, Kings, etc.). You could order this book via the Harvest Book Company, 800-669-2660, ext. 265. Note: Library of Congress card number, 58-7978.

9. *Choosing Schools: Consumer Choice and Quality of American Schools*, by Mark Schneider, Paul Teske, and Melissa Marschall, Princeton, NJ, Princeton University Press, 2002. Note: this excellent work is about elementary through high schools. Www.pupress.princeton.edu.

10. *History of Universities*, Vol. XIV, 1995–1996, by Charles Schmitt, Oxford University Press, Oxford, England, 1998.

11. *Higher Education in American Society,*, 3rd ed., 1994, by Philip G. Altbach, Robert O. Berdahl, and Patricia J. Gumport, Amherst, New York, N.Y. Prometheus Books.

12. *Community Colleges: Policy in the Future Context*, by Barbara K. Townsend and Susan B. Twombly, Westport, CT, Ablex Publishing, Division of Greenwood Publishing, 2001.

13. *Unlock the Einstein Inside: Applying New Brain Science to Wake Up the Smart in Your Child*, by Dr. Ken Gibson with Kim Hanson and Tanye Mitchell, 2nd ed., Colorado Springs, CO, Learning Rx™, 5085 List Drive, Suite 20, Colorado Springs, CO, 80919, 2007. Note: a unique book dealing in cognitive skills training, based on instruction in reading, math, and learning readiness.

14. *Cradles of Conscience: Ohio's Independent Colleges and Universities*, edited by John William Oliver Jr., James A. Hodges, and James H. O'Donnell, Kent, OH, The Kent State University Press, Kent & London, 2003. Note: a wonderful history of Ohio's historic and excellent liberal art colleges and universities.

15. *Imposters in the Temple: A Blueprint for Improving Higher Education in America*, by Martin Anderson, Stanford, CA, Hoover Press, 1996.

16. *Our Schools and Our Future ... Are We Still At Risk?*, by Paul E. Peterson, Editor, Stanford, CA, Hoover Press, 2003.

17. *Academic Heraldry in America*, by Kevin S. Heard, J.D., and illustrations by Paul Wainio, Marquette, MI, Northern Michigan College Press, The Book Concern, Hancock, MI, 1962.

# Notes

_____
_____
_____
_____
_____
_____
_____
_____
_____
_____
_____
_____
_____
_____
_____
_____
_____
_____
_____
_____
_____
_____

# Notes